ON BEING L.D.

Perspectives and Strategies
of Young Adults

Stephen T. Murphy

Teachers College, Columbia University
New York and London

Published by Teachers College Press, 1234 Amsterdam Avenue
New York, New York

Library of Congress Cataloging-in-Publication Data

Murphy, Stephen T.
    On being L.D. : perspectives and strategies of young adults /
Stephen T. Murphy.
        p.   cm. — (Special education series)
    Includes bibliographical references (p.) and index.
    ISBN 0-8077-3170-6 (alk. paper). — ISBN 0-8077-3169-2 (pbk. :
    alk. paper)
    1. Learning disabled youth—Education—United States.
2. Adjustment (Psychology) 3. Learning disabled—United States—
Interviews. I. Title. II. Series: Special education series (New
York, N.Y.)
LC4705.M86   1992
371.9—dc20   92-4945
    .

Printed on acid-free paper

Manufactured in the United States of America

99 98 97 96 95 94 93 92   8 7 6 5 4 3 2 1

This book is dedicated
to Mary Scott and Tom Murphy

———————————————————

Contents

Preface

The headline of a recent *Wall Street Journal* (1990) article proclaimed, "Scientists Find Gene That Can Cause Skin Tumors and Learning Disabilities." A similar theme was sounded several years earlier in the *Syracuse Herald-Journal*, where a letter to the editor was titled, "Learning Disabilities Are Real." The premise of both articles is that students who fail in school are not necessarily incompetent, lazy, or victims of bad teaching. They could have an organic disorder.

The conclusion that some people who do poorly in school have genetic and/or central nervous system disorders (Biller & White, 1989) is drawn regularly in schools across the country, where about 5% of *all school-age children*, and 43% of those diagnosed as handicapped, carry a label of learning disabled (Growick & Dowdy, 1989). In such instances intellectually normal children who fail to acquire basic academic skills are thought to have (a) developmental disorders of language, speech, reading, or communication; (b) learning process deficits involving perception, conception, or expression; and/or (c) psychological or neurological impairments of spoken or written language, or of perceptual, cognitive, or motor behavior (Lambert, 1986). Some experts have claimed that *50% of all school-age children* may have some sort of learning disabilities (see Senf, 1987).

The pairing of intellectual deficits, school failure, and physiogenic deficiencies is certainly not new (see Gould, 1982; Wolfensberger, 1975, for historical accounts of this perspective), and has been vigorously and thoroughly challenged over the years (see Coles, 1987; Gould, 1982; Kavale & Forness, 1985). McGuinness (1986) and other writers, however, have argued that national incidence figures reflect a renewed, a priori presumption that students identified as low achieving have some physiogenic dysfunction. Critics of such a tendency have contended that there is no more basis now than there ever was to claim that poor academic performance is caused by physiogenic defects. Believing that learning disabilities are based on unverified physiogenic states, and conferred through subjective, ill-defined criteria, they have argued that so-called learning disabled behaviors could be caused by a variety of undetermined sources, and are, for the most part, indistinguishable from behaviors of non-learning-disabled persons.

The purpose of this book is not to resolve the question of whether learning disabilities are real physiogenic entities or socially constructed myths. Rather, the intent is to reveal the experiences of people labeled learning disabled and to broaden the perspectives of those who study the concept and treat the problem. Examining the ways people with learning disabilities define themselves and their circumstances will enable us to better understand important referents for individual conduct. Moreover, by studying how individuals manage the educational, social, familial, and vocational demands of their everyday lives, we can more thoroughly uncover the adaptive and compensatory strategies they employ (Kavale, 1988), and more critically analyze existing theories, treatments, and public policies directed toward people with learning disabilities.

LEARNING ABOUT LEARNING DISABILITIES: METHODS OF STUDY

To find out how people classified as learning disabled perceived and managed the label, the author and a colleague conducted interviews of 49 adults upon whom the label had been formally conferred. All interviewees were referred to us by community professionals from whom we had asked for referrals, or by interviewees who had told a friend about the study. The interviews were unstructured initially, although as the interviewing progressed, a consistent series of open-ended questions was established and asked of each interviewee. Lists of these questions (Appendix A) and research themes and subthemes (Appendix B) appear at the end of the book. Each interview lasted for an average of an hour and 40 minutes. Interviewing times ranged from 55 minutes to 3½ hours.

Of the interviewees, 28 had been classified as learning disabled, general or nonspecific; 17 as dyslexic; and 4 as dysgraphic. A full complement of test data was not available on 8 students. Their records contained only letters from a psychologist, psychiatrist, or learning disabilities specialist, attesting to their designation as learning disabled. All individuals in the study had been diagnosed as learning disabled by a school or private psychologist or psychiatrist, or by a college learning disabilities diagnostician, and were judged eligible to receive special services and accommodations during their educational careers.

The average age of the 18 women and 34 men interviewed was 26 years. Their ages ranged from 19 to 47. All were white, and were attending, or had graduated from, either a 4-year college or a 2-year community or technical college. Thirty-four people attended or had graduated from a 4-year school, and 16 attended or had graduated from a 2-year college.

Two 4-year colleges and one 2-year college were selected as sources of interviewees because the facilities were known to have students with learning disabilities and a staff that would be receptive to the research. One 4-year college was a medium-sized university located in a medium-sized eastern city; the other was a small college located in a very rural area of the northeastern United States. At the university, students with learning disabilities comprised a small minority. At the small college, they constituted about one fourth of the total student population. The 2-year community college was also located in a medium-sized northern city and had a sizable number of students with learning disabilities and other academic problems. However, the students with diagnosed learning disabilities comprised a clear minority.

Students who had been receiving services and had been formally defined by their college as learning disabled were contacted and asked to be interviewed as part of a study on learning disabilities. The students were told that they would be asked to discuss how they viewed their disability and how they managed everyday school, family, social, and employment situations. All but one of the individuals contacted agreed to participate, and each signed a consent form attesting to their knowledge of the research and of their option to withdraw from the study at any time without prejudice. They also signed a release-of-information form, which secured their permission to publish their comments and assured them of anonymity. All of the interviews were tape recorded and transcribed, yielding over 1,200 pages of interviewing data.

The data were analyzed using a constant-comparative, emergent theme approach (see Glaser, 1978; Glaser & Strauss, 1967; Lofland, 1971). Following the transcription of each taped interview, the two principal investigators and a doctoral research associate (who also assisted with the interviewing) independently conducted a line-by-line analysis of each transcript, developing and recording subthemes identified from the interviews. Some examples of the themes included (a) strategies for revealing myself to instructors, (b) arranging my education and making it easier, (c) significant people who got me through college, (d) sizing people up, (e) revealing myself to employers, and

(f) passing and covering in classroom/employment situations. In total, over 200 subthemes were generated. These themes were then combined into about ten major themes, the five most comprehensive of which comprises four chapters of this book. The fifth theme, family issues, runs throughout the four chapters.

OUTLINE OF THE BOOK

Chapter 1 offers a brief historical account of the development of learning disabilities as an official societal handicap. Also contained in this chapter is a description of how the term came to be defined by contemporary researchers, educators, and parents; and a proposal for expanding the term conceptually, practically, and empirically.

Succeeding chapters describe how persons diagnosed as learning disabled perceived and dealt with the circumstances and people they encountered in their daily lives. Chapter 2 describes individuals' recollections of being diagnosed and their responses to that designation. Chapter 3 examines how persons managed the academic demands of school and college, including the various techniques and strategies they used to succeed in these settings. Chapter 4 addresses how people in school and college situations handled their social relationships with peers, and describes how learning disabilities affected people's social situations, how individuals managed information about themselves, and how people handled everyday social circumstances. Chapter 5 explores the social and task-related strategies people used to manage the employment world. Specifically described are the ways in which individuals prepared themselves for working, managed job interviews, dealt with troublesome work tasks and requirements, and handled relationships with supervisors and co-workers.

Initially there was to be a separate chapter on family issues. However, family issues were deeply rooted in people's activities and settings. Thus, the author decided to include family issues within the contexts in which people discussed them. In this way overlap was minimized, and the artificial separation of family involvements and dynamics from their appropriate contexts was eliminated. The activities of families are described in relation to diagnostic labeling, school and college functioning, social/peer relationships, and employment situations. The final chapter contains a summary of the important findings and their implications for professionals, families, individuals labeled learning disabled, and policy makers.

Acknowledgments ———————————————

The study on which this book is based was funded by a grant from the Syracuse University Senate Research Council. I greatly appreciated that funding and the availability of that kind of intra-university, faculty support.

I would especially like to acknowledge the critical assistance of Terry McDonald, who was instrumental in setting up and conducting interviews and in analyzing the findings. I am particularly indebted to all the people who volunteered to be interviewed, without whom the study on which this book is based could not have been completed.

Thanks to Doug Biklen, Peter Knoblock, Dwight Kauppi, and especially Faye Zuckerman and my longtime friend Mike Diamonti for their insightful editorial suggestions.

I am also very grateful to Bo Robertson for her long hours of coding work and discussions, and to Barb Pauley and Jeanne Sutliff for their help in the final stages of manuscript preparation.

Finally, I wish to express my gratitude for the assistance of my wife, Nancy, whose support and editorial help sustained me throughout the entire project, and the ceaseless interest of my children, Dan, Melissa, and Stacey, which kept me going during my frequent writing slumps.

1

Perspectives on Learning Disabilities

From modest beginnings, the learning disabilities concept has experienced a level of growth and application that Divorky described in 1974 as "awesome" (p. 23). And since then, formal incidences, public awareness, and professional recognition of learning disabilities have continued to increase dramatically. In 1970 120,000 public school students under the age of 21 were classified as learning disabled (Growick & Dowdy, 1989). According to the U.S. Office of Special Education's Eighth Annual Report to Congress, by 1986 this figure had risen to 1.75 million. This represents more than a 1,400% increase since 1970, and a doubling of incidence since 1975. Moreover, the number of children diagnosed as learning disabled represents 4½% of all students in our nation's schools, and encompasses 42% of the children assigned to special education programs across the U.S. With the inclusion of learning disabilities in the federal vocational rehabilitation legislation, the incidence of adults with learning disabilities is also projected to increase (Growick & Dowdy, 1989; Mars, 1986; Miller, Mulkey, & Kopp, 1984). Small wonder that Senf (1987, pp. 88–89) described the LD movement as growing from "anonymity and social disinterest to [become] the most prevalent handicapping condition in this country, all in less than 25 years."

The federal commitment to the learning disabilities movement is also reflected in the increased funding that has been allotted to the problem, particularly in relation to other handicapping conditions (McKinney, 1987). According to McKinney, the cost of special education programs in general has increased 14% per year (Keogh, 1987; Stark, 1982) since the implementation of P.L. 94-142, The Education For All Handicapped Children Act of 1975. This figure, which contrasts sharply with the 7% rise in regular education costs, has been attributed mainly to the inclusion of learning disabled students under P.L. 94-142 legislation.

Because of the 1981 vocational rehabilitation legislation, which made persons with learning disabilities eligible to receive state and federally funded employment services, the costs of serving adults classified as learning disabled are projected to increase appreciably. Until recently, relatively few persons with learning disabilities had received vocational rehabilitation services, and for those over the age of 25, such services have been almost nonexistent (Miller, Mulkey, & Kopp, 1984). However, recent analyses by the Rehabilitation Services Administration have shown a dramatic increase since 1983 in the numbers of persons served who have learning disabilities (Mars, 1986).

OFFICIAL DEFINITIONS AND PUBLIC POLICY

The Realist View

From a public policy perspective, learning disabilities have been described and treated as physiological and/or behavioral deficits that impede people's learning how to read, write, spell, and/or do math. This perspective best represents the way learning disabilities are defined and treated within special education and human service fields. It constitutes the basis for federal policy, informs practice in public schools and adult vocational rehabilitation programs, and serves as a conceptual and practical guide for researchers, parents, practitioners, and policy makers at all levels of government. Mehan, Hertweck, and Meihls (1986) have referred to this orientation as the "realist" perspective because learning disabilities are perceived as "brute facts," that is, *real* physiogenic, intra-individual anomalies. According to Mehan et al.:

> From a realist point of view, handicaps reside in students or in their conduct. . . . The medical metaphor has been extended from the physical to the mental domain within education. As a consequence, intelligence, aptitude, or mental ability have been medicalized and subject to treatment. It is this medical metaphor that leads to the view that students have a "problem." This problem is a disability perceived as residing in students, as their private, personal possession. (p. 159)

Underlying the learning disabilities movement is the belief that there exists a "true" form of learning disability that is not only neurogenic, but also is independent of any other disability or learning circumstance. This is not to say that learning disabilities cannot exist in combination with other identified disabilities (although some definitions deny or ignore this possibility). It is to say that a person's learning problem, to be considered truly a learning disability, cannot be the result of another disability or of factors extrinsic to the person. This belief is perhaps best described by Kirk (1987), a leading advocate for the existence of a "pure" learning disability:

> The field of learning disabilities (LD), originally associated with severe problems in learning resulting from a neurologic deficit, has in practice become primarily concerned with academic under-achievement at the school-age level. [There are] two major reasons for underachievement: (1) extrinsic or environmental factors, and (2) intrinsic or internal factors. The intrinsic factors . . . include mental retardation, sensory handicaps, serious emotional distur-bance, and LD.
>
> The concept of LD . . . involves an intrinsic disability within the child that has inhibited the child's ability to learn under ordinary instruction. LD are academic disabilities resulting from develop-mental disabilities such as memory, perception, attention, thinking, or language. These developmental disabilities . . . later manifest themselves as disabilities in reading, spelling, handwriting, written expression and mathematics. The intervention . . . will require reme-diation that ameliorates the developmental deficit during the pro-cess of teaching the academic subjects. (pp. 173, 175)

The preceding quotation exemplifies the realist orientation within the field's practice. Such an orientation also exists within the field's research agenda, where inquirers are exhorted to capture the essence of learning disabilities by differentiating the "true LDs" from the "impostors" (McGrady, 1987, p. 108). Moreover, investigators conduct their inquiries under rubrics such as information processing and neuro-psychology, differentiate between learning disabled and non-learning-disabled persons, study observable neurological or behavioral differ-ences, and compare treatment effects between delineated groups (Vaughn, Bos, & Kucik, 1987).

A neurogenic/realist view of learning disabilities appears to tran-scend any current theoretical positions within the field. Whereas ad-herents of psychological process, behavioral, and/or cognitive learn-ing models have expressed little interest in the neurogenic etiology debates (see Brown & Campione, 1986; Poplin, 1985), their emphasis upon skill acquisition and behavioral generalization underscores their realist orientation toward learning disabilities. As Poplin (1985) has contended, adherents of these models all place the problem and their interventions squarely in the lap of the individual, because it is most frequently the student's behavior that becomes the focus of skill acquisition and generalization training.

Realist Underpinnings of Formal Definitions

Hammill (1990) identified eleven different definitions of learning disabilities "which are prominent today or that experienced some degree of popularity at one time" (p. 75). He contended that of the eleven, only four are professionally viable today. In the following discussion three definitions of learning disabilities are presented. The three were selected because they have gained widespread prominence within the field, illustrate important conceptual differences, and/or serve as the basis for admission to special educational or vocational services.

The U.S. Office of Education (USOE) definition, described within P.L. 94-142, has been adopted by most state education departments as a guide to identifying learning disabled students within this nation's schools. Within this definition a learning disability is described as a:

> disorder of one or more of the basic psychological processes involved in understanding or using language, spoken or written, which may manifest itself in an imperfect ability to listen, think, speak, read, write, spell, or do mathematical calculations. The term includes such conditions as perceptual handicaps, brain injury, minimal brain dysfunction, dyslexia, and developmental aphasia. The term does not include children who have learning problems which are primarily the result of visual, hearing, or motor handicaps, of mental retardation, of emotional disturbance, or of environmental, cultural, or economic disadvantage. (§ 5B-4)

In 1981 an alternative to the USOE definition was proposed by the National Joint Committee for Learning Disabilities (NJCLD). This definition, modified somewhat in 1988, stated that:

> Learning disability is a generic term that refers to a heterogeneous group of disorders manifested by significant difficulties in the acquisition and use of listening, speaking, reading, writing and reasoning, or mathematical abilities. These disorders are intrinsic to the individual, presumed to be due to central nervous system dysfunctions, and may occur across the life span. Problems in self-regulatory behaviors, social perception, and social interactions may exist with learning disabilities but do not by themselves constitute a learning disabil-

ity. Although learning disabilities may occur concomitantly with other handicapping conditions (for example, sensory impairment, mental retardation, seriouis emotional disturbance) or with extrinsic influences (such as cultural differences, insufficient or inappropriate instruction), they are not the result of these conditions or influences. (NJCLD, 1988, p. 1)

The NJCLD definition departed somewhat from the federal description, by attempting to minimize what were considered nebulous, confusing phrases such as "basic psychological processes, perceptual handicaps," and "minimal brain dysfunction." Included in this definition were adults as well as children, and excluded were specific reference to spelling and the requirement that learning disabilities could occur only in the absence of other disabilities (Hallahan, Kauffman, & Lloyd, 1985, p. 14; Hammill, 1990). It should be noted, however, that the NJCLD definition retained the physiogenic, intra-individual and (basically) exclusionary components of previous definitions (see Kavale & Forness, 1985; Kolligan & Sternberg, 1987).

The influence of the physiogenic/intra-individual view of learning disabilities was illustrated most dramatically in the process through which state and federally funded vocational rehabilitation organizations (VR) arrived at an acceptance and definition of learning disabilities as an official disability, and as a basis for receiving adult services. Newell, Goyette, and Fogarty (1984) reported that for years vocational rehabilitation agencies were under pressure to serve individuals with learning disabilities. However, VR administrators resisted such inclusion because the label had no medical standing. To meet the VR criteria, persons claiming to be learning disabled had to demonstrate medical evidence of neurological impairment. This requirement proved unsatisfactory for many people who could not confirm their disability in this way.

In 1980, however, learning disabilities received full medical approval with inclusion in the American Psychiatric Association's (1980) *Diagnostic and Statistical Manual of Mental Disorders*, 3rd edition (DSM III), and in the World Health Organization's *International Classification of Diseases* (1980). Thus, in 1981, the Rehabilitation Services Administration (RSA) permitted classification of learning disabilities as a mental disorder, and eligibility for adults so certified who also met the agency's general criteria for services.

In 1985 RSA officials again changed their definition of learning disabilities from that of an exclusively mental disorder to a neuropsychological dysfunction. This reasserted the neurogenic basis of learning disabilities, yet enabled a person to be classified using psychologically based methodologies (Biller & White, 1989). Specifically, the VR definition refers to learning disabilities as:

> a disorder in one or more of the central nervous system processes involved in perceiving, understanding, and/or using concepts through verbal (spoken) or written language or nonverbal means. This disorder manifests itself with a deficit in one or more areas: attention, reasoning, processing, memory, communication, reading, spelling, writing, calculation, coordination, social competence, and emotional maturity. (Rehabilitation Services Administration, PPD-85-7, 1985)

The realist perspective is clearly evident within the VR definition, both conceptually (as noted above) and operationally. Operationally, people are certified as learning disabled within VR agencies if an accredited professional verifies that they have (a) average or above average intelligence, (b) a discrepancy between ability and achievement, (c) central nervous system dysfunction, (d) an absence of other primary disabilities (Mulkey, Kopp, & Miller, 1984), and/or (e) evidence of social incompetence or social immaturity (Biller & White, 1989).

CONTROVERSIAL PERSPECTIVES

Despite its many proponents, and its widespread application, the term *learning disabilities* is surrounded by controversy. Much of the controversy has centered around the origins and validity of the label, the narrow way in which it has been defined, and its value as a clinical designation. Besides the multiple definitions noted by Hammill (1990) and described earlier, Chalfant (1989) found that five criteria have been used to designate learning disabled students, and that states and school districts employ different combinations of these criteria to classify students. Keogh (1988) and Chalfant (1989) also have observed that in part because of these diagnostic inconsistencies, an increasing number of professionals have begun to question the continued use of the learning disabilities label. Although it is beyond the scope of this chapter to provide an exhaustive review of these controversies, in the next section we will examine briefly some of the criticisms that have been leveled at the learning disabilities phenomenon (for more complete reviews see Coles, 1987; Kavale, 1988; Kavale & Forness, 1985; Keogh, 1988; Poplin, 1985; and Skrtic, 1986).

Identifying the Political Constituency

Critics of the concept of learning disabilities have indicated that, historically, learning disabilities have been as closely affiliated with politics as with science. As nearly every textbook on learning disabilities has noted, the term *learning disabilities* was coined by Samuel Kirk, a university professor of special education, during a 1963 speech at the Fund for the Perceptually Handicapped Conference held in Chicago. The conference was reportedly called by parents who during the 1950s and early 1960s were attempting to secure services for their low-achieving but otherwise normal children. For numerous reasons these parents refused to label their children mentally retarded, and were often frustrated because their children were ineffectively taught in regular classes, were not provided necessary services without being assigned unduly stigmatizing labels, and were often inappropriately placed in special education classes for students with sensory, emotional, or more serious mental disabilities. As Lerner (1985) concluded, it was this perceived neglect of children who appeared to be normal, but who had specific kinds of learning problems for which there were no services, that stimulated parent groups to take political action.

It was clear that parental and professional leaders attending the Chicago conference desired to establish a new disability category and a new, broad-based political constituency around this disability. At the time there existed a strong tradition of linking learning problems with brain dysfunction, a tendency that could be traced to the research of Orton, Strauss, Werner, and their associates (Kavale & Forness, 1985; Kolligan & Sternberg, 1987). The term *brain-injured*, however, received little support from Kirk and the other conference participants as a way of describing children with learning problems. To gain public, political, and professional recognition, acceptance, and support for their cause, they needed a label that was broader than reading or mathematics disability, different from other mental disabilities, and less stigmatizing than mental retardation, emotional disturbance, or brain-injured (Lerner, 1985, p. 34; McGuinness, 1986, pp. 5–6). However, despite the sociopolitical rejection of the phrase brain-injured, they accepted the idea of learning disabilities as a manifestation of neurological dysfunction and built the foundation upon which the field was constructed and continues to rest (Kavale & Forness, 1985; Wiederholt, 1974).

The link between learning disabilities and neurological dysfunction has persisted despite the contradictions that inhere in the linkage and the criticisms that have surrounded it. Kavale and Forness (1985) have provided a convincing argument against this linkage, and numerous other writers have pointed out that the concept of learning disabilities as a neurogenic entity is far from settled. Kolligan and Sternberg (1987, p. 8) have related, for example, that:

> The puzzle (of domain specific deficits) is inherent in the definition of specific learning disabilities: This definition refers to individuals who have a deficit in a specific domain of intellectual functioning, such as reading, calculating, or spelling, yet also have average or above-average general intelligence. It should be noted that whereas disabled individuals lack specific abilities, the converse is not necessarily true; not all individuals who lack specific abilities are learning disabled. Furthermore, we consider a learning disability to be an "intrinsic deficit, one not caused by (but perhaps exacerbated by) external factors such as poor teaching . . . or other handicapping conditions, such as sensory impairment or emotional disturbance (Spear & Sternberg, 1986, p. 3)."

Critics of the learning disabilities movement have referred to it as a blatant example of social scientists uncritically mixing politics and science, and ignoring the conceptual and empirical contradictions that have confronted them. Gould (1982, pp. 22–23) has articulately described how and why such uncritical thinking can occur within the scientific community, arguing that scientists have social, cultural, economic, psychological, and political dispositions that color which problems they study, the way they study them, the results they obtain, and the conclusions they draw:

> Science . . . is a socially embedded activity. It progresses by hunch, vision, and intuition. Much of its change through time does not record a closer approach to absolute truth, but the alteration of cultural contexts that influence it so strongly. . . . I believe that a factual reality exists, and that science, often in an obtuse and erratic manner, can learn about it. . . . Yet the history of many scientific subjects is virtually free from . . . constraints of fact for two major reasons: First, some topics are invested with enormous social importance, but blessed with very little reliable information. . . . Second, many questions are formulated by scientists in such a restricted way that any legitimate answer can only validate a social preference. (pp. 22–23)

Put more succinctly by Foster, Yesseldyke, and Reese, "If they hadn't believed it, they wouldn't have seen it" (1975, p. 469).

Mehan, Hertweck, and Meihls (1986, pp. 159–161) have claimed that advocates of the concept of learning disabilities have reified intelligence, educational potential, and academic performance into medical conditions and assigned meaning, value, and etiology to these terms depending upon a student's assessed intelligence/performance profile. Gould (1982) explained the fallacies and potential dangers of reification as it relates to the concept of intelligence:

> The argument begins with one of the fallacies—reification or our tendency to convert abstract concepts into entities. . . . Once intelligence becomes an entity, standard procedures of science virtually dictate that a location and physical substrate be sought for it. Since the brain is the seat of mentality, intelligence must reside there. We recognize the importance of mentality in our lives and wish to characterize it, in part, so that we can make the divisions and distinctions among people that our cultural and political systems dictate.
>
> We now encounter the second fallacy—ranking, or our propensity for ordering complex variation as a gradual ascending scale. Ranking requires a criterion for assigning all individuals to their proper status in the single series. And what better criterion than an objective number. (p. 24)

As Gould, Mehan, and others have indicated, intelligence is seldom related to health or physiological pathology. These authors have argued, however, that such linkages make political sense in a society where decisions about persons must be made every day and where science is king. According to these critics, constructing educational potential/performance profiles and linking them with medicine and psychology is a way of legitimating, accounting for, and controlling individual differences as personal deficiencies.

Narrowing the Field of Treatment

Caplan and Nelson (1973, p. 200) have noted that what is done about a problem depends on how it is defined, and that such definitions are based on assumptions about the causes of the problem. Moreover, such definitions tend to characterize problems indefinitely, to reflect existing sociocultural values and myths, and to influence the self-concepts, expectations, and behavior of people to whom the definitions are applied. Those who fault the learning disabilities concept contend that its definition perpetuates a restrictive, person-blame interpretation of school failure; minimizes the cultural, political, and institutional sources of people's learning problems; and contributes to the development of unduly narrow treatment approaches (Kavale & Forness, 1985; Lambert, 1986; Mehan et al., 1986; Poplin, 1985; Skrtic, 1986).

It is generally taken for granted by human service researchers and practitioners that definitions of disability and the treatment techniques that follow them are based on objective, scientific information, and that such definitions and programs operate in the best interests of those people to whom they apply. Numerous writers have pointed out, however, that this is not always the case. Social scientists have long recognized that every society attempts to characterize its deviant members as a source of problems, and therefore as targets of change. According to Becker (1963), Friedson (1965), Lane (1977), Caplan and Nelson (1973), and others, person-centered interpretations of social problems may serve a variety of latent social control functions, tend to blame people in difficult situations for their own predicament, and often operate in everyone's interests except those subjected to analysis.

Because of this societal tendency to view narrowly such social problems as learning disabilities, human service researchers and practitioners who want their work to be recognized as useful and relevant are under pressure to study and treat social problems in primarily person-centered terms. Researchers in particular have been criticized for heeding the "banal call for usefulness," for joining the "cult of individualism," and for uncritically accepting "person-blame causal definitions of a problem and avoiding a systems analysis" (Lane, 1977, p. 1057). As Lane has argued:

> Context refers to the interrelation of a variety of structured milieux in our immediate environment, such as the family unit, agencies of education, health, recreation, [law enforcement], and business, as they currently exist, their historical development, and their future evolution. As experiencing living individuals, we are continuously aware of the tremendously controlling influence of an array of such corporate bodies. We know these bodies do not exist independently of one another, but continuously interact and modify each other. . . . As researchers, however, we persist in conceptualizing human behavior as primarily determined by enduring and consistent characteristics of the individual. (pp. 1056–1057)

Critics have charged that within the learning disabilities field, situation-centered, causal factors that emanate from the larger social, cultural, and political arena are excluded from consideration as causes of learning disabilities. However, as Mehan et al. (1986) discovered, whereas student behaviors varied within schools, a consistent process of student labeling occurred that depended upon (a) the meanings school professionals and parents attached to such behaviors, and (b) the context surrounding student behaviors and professional-student behavior. Despite these and similar findings (see Rist, 1973; Rosenthal & Jacobson, 1968), the individual remains the predominant target in the fight against learning problems. Researchers and practitioners perpetuate the narrow scope of treatment by failing to assess, address, alter, or circumvent the social, political, and cultural causes and contexts of "disability" (Skrtic, 1986).

Poplin (1985) has referred to the field's narrow focus as a reductionist fallacy:

> The methods we currently apply . . . are all examples of erroneously believing that a complex whole such as human learning or learning problems can be broken into its component parts (e.g., neural processes, hypothetical psychological processes, . . . observable academic and social behaviors, and cognitive or learning strategies) in order to design more effective practice in assessment and instruction.
>
> In the case of the medical and psychological process model, the problem lay clearly in the student's aberrant processing of information. This orientation is not unlike that of the (cognitive) strategists. . . . The behaviorists, while disclaiming to discredit the student with the disability, still define the intervention as the careful and conscious modification of the *student's behaviors* through the manipulation of the external environment. But let us not forget that the desired *change* in each model lies *within* the student even though the designated *agent* of change may be teacher or school. (p. 394)

Assigning Stigma and Labeling Deviance

A third criticism of the realist orientation toward learning disabilities is that it often exacerbates the stigma associated with a person's learning problems. To realists there exists a world of troubled, underachieving, medically dysfunctional students out there who need to be identified, assessed, and treated (Mehan et al., 1986, p. 159; Poplin, 1984, 1985). As described by White (1985, p. 231), many unwitting individuals in our society could benefit from being diagnosed and treated as learning disabled: "millions of [persons with learning disabilities] struggle with the sometimes overwhelming trials of daily life without knowing why they are different from their friends and neighbors, or how to overcome their problems." Hewitt (1984), Lambert (1986), and McGuinness (1986) have pointed out, however, that a fundamental consequence of applying to people such labels as learning disabilities is the assignment of those people to categories of inferiority. Learning disabilities, mental illness, and alcoholism are more than categories of problem behaviors. They are designations in which people are viewed as "less than normal, not up to normal human capabilities or dispositions" (Hewitt, 1984, p. 239). Moreover, the application of these definitions determines how targeted people are understood and treated in everyday situations.

Critics have argued that people with learning disabilities have been assigned a label by others, usually professionals, who define abnormality by the degree to which an individual statistically varies from the norm of a population in specific behavioral characteristics. Because learning disabilities are assumed to reflect neurogenic dysfunction (even though they almost always occur in the absence of any physiological signs of pathology), the model of measurement becomes transposed with the pathogenic model of medicine. Consequently, statistical signs are used to denote dysfunction, individual differences become interpreted as pathology, and individuals are treated as if they were sick (Mehan et al., 1986; Skrtic, 1986; Mercer, 1973).

Poplin (1984, 1985) has argued that within a pathology orientation such as that described above, the remedial emphasis is always on what is wrong with the person, and what the student has failed to learn. She states further that students labeled as learning disabled must spend twice as much time as their nondisabled peers practicing what they do poorly, thereby minimizing or negating the talents and interests they may have. Biklen and Zollers (1986) support such a critique, adding that many schools employ a "pull-out model" to treat students with learning disabilities, removing them from the regular classroom to a segregated class. This not only separates them from their friends, but also assigns them a devalued status in relation to their peers during a developmental period characterized by acute self-consciousness and the need for social acceptance.

Critics have also pointed out that physiogenic pathology has not been the only stigma linked to learning disabilities. The condition has also been closely, if not causally, linked to other stigmatizing states such as emotional disturbance and criminality.

Numerous studies link learning disabilities to social and emotional problems. Experts have indicated that persons with learning disabilities exhibit social and emotional behaviors that are both serious and long-term (see Adelman & Taylor, 1983; Gresham, 1988; Hallahan,

Kauffman, & Lloyd, 1985; Kavale, 1988; Lerner, 1981; Mercer, 1987). Gresham (1988), Hallahan et al. (1985, pp. 140–146), and Kavale (1988) have noted that learning disabled children have been found to exhibit inattentive and hyperactive behaviors that reflect and/or cause social and emotional problems, and hamper social acceptance and emotional adjustment into adulthood. Among the most frequently cited social and emotional symptoms attributed to persons with learning disabilities are hyperactivity, distractibility, low self-concept, social skill deficits, impulsivity, disruptiveness, withdrawal, dependency, perseveration, and failure to develop friendships and to get along with adults.

Common characteristics

Learning disabilities have also been linked to juvenile delinquency (see Berman, 1981; Berman & Siegal, 1976; Mauser, 1974; Poremba, 1975; Wilgosh & Paitich, 1982). As Lane (1980) observed, this association flowed easily from common sense views regarding the causes and consequences of these two social problems: "The theoretical proposition that a causal link exists between learning disabilities and juvenile delinquency appears to be the natural and logical product of the matching of these two school failure related concepts" (p. 20).

Several government-sponsored research projects have examined what has been termed the "LD-JD link." No clear relationship emerged from these studies. In fact, in one study conducted by Murray (1976), and sponsored jointly by the Law Enforcement Assistance Administration and the National Institute for Juvenile Justice and Delinquency Prevention, evidence for a causal link was described as feeble. However, studies have emerged that point to an LD-JD linkage. Murray, for example, while rejecting a *causal* relationship between learning disabilities and juvenile delinquency, concluded, using qualitative data, that a broad *pattern* of learning disabilities may exist among juvenile delinquents. Moreover, a 1977 investigation conducted by the General Accounting Office, and cited by Lane (1980), found that all of the juveniles studied had significant learning problems. In a third federally sponsored study, the National Association for Children with Learning Disabilities (ACLD) Research and Demonstration Project (1978), it was concluded that 32% of adjudicated delinquents had learning disabilities, as opposed to 16% of nonadjudicated school children.

While studying and finding linkages between learning disabilities and socially maladaptive behavior, numerous researchers have indicated that not everyone with learning disabilities who exhibits dysfunctional behavior incurs social or emotional problems, or engages in delinquent behavior. Researchers have noted further that such behaviors are frequently manifested by persons who are not learning disabled, and are often related to environmental factors. Research linking these disorders is abundant, however, and as Lane (1980) has stated, such linkage, however vague, has left in the minds of many the lingering perception of a JD-LD association.

A BROADENED PERSPECTIVE ON LEARNING DISABILITIES

The concept of learning disabilities is surrounded by controversy and debate. The term has been called more political than scientific, more societal than individual, and more stigmatizing than helpful. The ambiguity and amorphousness of the term seems underscored by the various ways it is defined across settings and audiences (Chalfant, 1988; Keogh, 1988). In fact, what may be most common among people labeled learning disabled is not so much a set of predictable, measurable biological or behavioral attributes, but the act of definition itself (Friedson, 1965).

But what of the people who have been defined as learning disabled? Do they view their label and its attendant associations as more political than scientific, more medical than systemic, more helpful or hurtful? What role do they play in determining their diagnosis? And how do they manage their own classification, their lives, and the people, tasks, and situations that confront them?

Labeled individuals are often portrayed as passive recipients of their designations. However, Levitin (1975) and others have argued that the role of individuals designated as deviant has been largely understated or ignored. According to the author, such persons "tend to be presented as passive or reactive, rather than as active agents in the labeling process" (Levitin, 1975, p. 548). Levitin goes on to ask why "the self-conceptions of the deviating individual should not be considered a crucial *independent* variable?"

The Insider's View

In the following section an attempt will be made to discuss the person with learning disabilities as active agent, and describe briefly a way of looking at his or her experiences from what Dembo (1970), Wright (1983), and Schneider and Conrad (1985) have called the "inside" perspective. Very little investigative attention has been paid to studying learning disabilities from the vantage point of those who have been so labeled. Numerous writers, however, have attested that an inside perspective will provide much needed depth to our understanding of the learning disabilities experience, and of the societal treatments and policies that have been designated as remediation. Becker (1966, p. 51) has urged the pursuit of such a perspective as a way to heighten understanding of "ourselves, our society, and the value of the label." Supporting this view, Matza (1969), Clinard and Meier (1985), and Ponte (1974) observed that people defined as deviant frequently see the world differently than do those who are not outsiders. These authors pointed to the interactive nature of labeling, warning that unless researchers and practitioners attend to the subjects' definition of the situation, comprehend their views, and interpret the world as it appears to them, then the social definitions, labels, and treatments professionals create "from the outside become difficult to maintain, since they achieve little prominence in the interpretations and definitions of persons in daily life" (Ponte, 1974, p. 117).

Despite the evident importance of self-reported descriptions, the perceptions of individuals classified as learning disabled remain largely undocumented. Some self-reported material has been described. In a study by Cruickshank, Morse, and Johns (1980), young adults described their experiences growing up with learning disabilities. However, the number of interviewees was very small, and no attempt was made to collate descriptions according to unifying themes or broader issues.

Schneider (1984) interviewed 26 LD students ages 10–20 who were enrolled in a Canadian residential school for children with severe learning disabilities. The author focused on how the interviewees perceived their disabilities and their placement at the school, and how they managed their interpersonal relations. According to Schneider the students liked their placement at the school, although he noted that few of them seemed to understand that they were learning disabled or what learning disabilities were. Regarding friendships, the author stated that interviewees reportedly had friends, that they spoke of a few close friends and indicated that their friends understood them. The author noted, however, that interviewees apparently did not tell peers in their home communities about their problems or about the school they were attending.

Although Schneider focused on some very important and interesting areas of study, he reported only global themes and provided few specific details about these areas. For example, whereas students reportedly liked their placement in the residential school, it would have been interesting to know how they understood the placement, what they liked about it, and how they described it to others. In addition, it would have been informative to know what kinds of specific strategies they used to manage the academic demands of the school, how they compared their past and present schools, and how their families described to them their academic problems and their placement in a special school. Also, although it is useful to know that interviewees avoided telling friends at home about their learning disabilities and about the school they attended, it would have been even more interesting to know exactly how they did this: what they said about their learning disabilities and their school in order to conceal or minimize their stigma, and how and what they told their friends at home.

Buchanan and Wolf (1986) collected personal and educational histories and test data of 33 adults with learning disabilities, noting that few systematic studies of either a descriptive or experimental nature have been reported in the literature. Like Schneider, the authors concluded that their interviewees possessed little understanding of their learning disabilities and the effects of these problems on their lives.

Buchanan and Wolf also reported that people identified their problems in terms such as low motivation, distractibility, low self-concept, emotional lability, and lack of organization. Like earlier writers, however, Buchanan and Wolf did not explain what interviewees meant by the terms they used, or illustrate how these terms concretely applied to specific school, social, and/or work situations.

There have been numerous large sample surveys of young adults with learning disabilities (see Hoffman et al., 1987; Polloway, Smith, & Patton, 1988; Zigmond & Thornton, 1985). Many of these studies were designed to identify the needs of this population and/or to associate personal or educational characteristics with particular postsecondary outcomes. Whereas these investigations have focused on such important characteristics as type of learning disability, level of education, and self-concept, and such important outcomes as college and employment success, life satisfaction, and successful social relationships, they have failed to include in sufficient depth the perceptions of those who have been labeled learning disabled. Of particular importance has been the failure of researchers to really explore how persons called learning disabled have operationally defined school, social, and employment experiences, self-concept, and life satisfactions; and how they have confronted or denied and avoided these experiences and issues in everyday situations.

In several of the preceding studies, researchers concluded that persons with learning disabilities did not know much about their disabilities. Other studies indicate, however, that persons with disabilities do understand their situations, but in ways that are different than those proposed by professionals (Dembo, 1970; Murphy, 1988; Murphy

& Salomone, 1983; Rosenhan, 1973). It appears that researchers must be wary of any tendency to discount, however inadvertently, people's perspectives of their situations; avoid behaving as if there is a *right* definition for such circumstances; and carefully examine such disparities when they appear.

One study that did focus on such professional-client disparities was conducted by Hoffman et al. (1987). They surveyed 381 adults with learning disabilities, 942 professional service providers, and 212 service consumers (parents and advocates) regarding the needs of adults with learning disabilities. The researchers asked members of each group to identify problems the learning disabled were having in several areas, such as academics, cognitive processing, medicine and health, social skills, personal issues, delinquency, and employment. The researchers found that persons with learning disabilities held different perceptions of these problems than did providers and consumers. As for academics, learning disabled adults reported having difficulties with reading, spelling, written composition, and handwriting, whereas providers and consumers identified only reading as a significant adult problem. Providers and consumers viewed learning disabled adults as having more significant social problems than did the learning disabled adults themselves. Specifically, providers and consumers saw young adults with learning disabilities as having more difficulties making friends and tending to become more dependent on others than did their nondisabled peers. Regarding personal problems, providers and consumers believed that adults with learning disabilities had the most problems with feelings of frustration and lack of self-confidence; the young adults wtih learning disabilities also felt that they had problems in these three areas, but saw them as less serious. The young adults also believed that they had far less trouble controlling their actions than providers and consumers thought they did.

A Phenomenological View

A fact of American educational life is that some otherwise capable students do poorly in school. For no detectable reason, they are unable to read, write, spell, or do mathematics as well as expected. As reflected by the comments of persons in this book, such individuals become demoralized and may withdraw or behave aggressively. A painful reality for them is that they fail to fit in, or measure up to whatever expectations are applied to them by themselves or others. As one person in the study stated, "The message my family was getting and giving to me was that I'm smart, but I'm pretty stupid."

The growing rate at which students are being identified as learning disabled, combined with federal and state legislation that has defined learning disabilities as an official handicap, and parental pressure for more and better services for their children, have led to a multitude of research and treatment programs intended to better identify and alleviate what is understood as the learning disabilities problem (see Deschler, Schumaker, & Lenz, 1984; Johnston, 1984; White, 1985). However, in the rush to predict, identify, and control learning disabilities, researchers have minimized the importance of the social, subjective, and phenomenological aspects of this designation. Undocumented are what Schneider and Conrad (1985, p. 9) have referred to as the "personal, detailed contours of people's lives, lived with and in spite of, disability." Increasing our knowledge of such "inside" perceptions through a phenomenological approach holds much promise for broadening our narrow, and much maligned, conceptual understanding of learning disabilities, and for developing more meaningful and effective services for people who have been called learning disabled.

The research orientation of a phenomenological/interactionist approach is different from that of traditional social science inquiry. Insofar as researchers are focusing on the various meanings people attach to phenomena such as learning disabilities, they are no longer preoccupied with disabled behavior, causation, and/or differences between disabled and nondisabled persons. As Sharp and Green (1975) have stated:

> Clearly, such an approach to social reality is very different from one which sees societies as embodying mechanistic or causal relationships. The stress which this perspective lays on the creative, knowing subject, and his ability through symbolic communication with others, to create both himself and his world brings the individual right into the forefront of history and society. The rejection of mechanistic determinism makes the search for causal regularities either at the psychological level or at the social level inappropriate.
>
> The task [for the researcher] is therefore to provide an ongoing description of the flow of phenomena in the consciousness of social actors. It requires that we explore the way in which social actors define their situations, their subjective typifications of themselves and others, and the rules which define how reality is subjectively [determined] and experienced in [social] settings. (p. 20)

The views of people with learning disabilities afford one perspective from which to examine the concept of learning disabilities. These views have value in their own right, and may be studied independently of consensual accounts of what exists or happens. They comprise important referents for individual conduct and permit greater understanding of people's experiences and behavior, including their reactions to the services they receive.

As Skrtic (1986) has argued, the inclusion of alternative conceptions of disability into treatment modalities is not just a technical point, but a moral obligation:

> Once one accepts the position that special education and "disability" can be viewed in alternative ways, and more important, that each perspective has different implications for children labeled disabled and their parents and families, the argument that special education *should* consider itself and its professional knowledge from alternative vantage points is self-evident on ethical and moral grounds. For special education to continue to rely on an exclusively biological/psychological explanation of "disability" has no defensible argument. (p. 6)

The major objective of this book is to provide an alternative, detailed view of the learning disabilities experience from the insider's standpoint. Studying the practical, working definition that labeled people develop and act on in the course of their everyday lives will enable us to better understand the concept we call learning disabilities, critically analyze our own practices and policies toward persons with learning problems, and develop ways of assistance that go beyond official definitions and reflect broadened, alternative perspectives.

Not Measuring Up:
Being Labeled Learning Disabled

CIRCUMSTANCES SURROUNDING THE LABEL

Great variability has characterized the learning disabled designation. As indicated by people's comments, individuals were labeled at different ages, in different places, by different people, for different reasons. Persons who described similar symptoms and educational experiences were defined as learning disabled in one school and not another, by one teacher and/or professional and not another, in one family and not another, even by one parent and not another. In addition, persons of very different achievement levels were diagnosed as learning disabled, ranging from people who had almost failed first grade or who had stayed back two or three times, to individuals who had graduated from law school, or who were successfully completing medical school, or who had graduated from high school at age 16 with honors.

Despite such diversity, one common thread that ran through the results was that learning disabilities were indigenous to educational settings. People almost always reported being labeled in school, or as a result of poor school performance. Of the 49 interviewees, 39 were reportedly identified by, or referred for testing by, school or college professionals. The remainder were identified by parents, family friends, or community professionals. Two were self-referred. No one reported being labeled before entering school, and only one individual indicated that she had been classified as a result of noneducational activities. That one person had referred herself for testing after a job experience, believing that something was wrong with her. She explained: "On that job there were two of us hired at the same time and she was learning it quicker than I was. I thought I was losing my mind."

Acquiring the Label

Another important theme that ran through people's comments was the sentiment of "not measuring up." Measuring up was defined as the degree to which persons met their own educational expectations and/or those of their parents, teachers, and school. As was implied earlier, measuring up was a relative term that parents, schools, and teachers defined differently, accounting for the different diagnostic patterns people described.

At school. Those who did not measure up at school often came to be looked upon as puzzles or as people with problems, despite how normal they may hitherto have been considered by friends, family, or teachers. One respondent recalled being considered talented before his school performance dropped:

> Everyone looked at me and was amazed by my conversational and thinking ability, which shocked even my father who graduated college at 19. They saw that I was getting Cs and Ds in school, and they wanted to know why. And that's when I went through all the testing.

Another person reported that between his high social abilities and low school performance, he was considered by his teachers, family, and friends as a "contradiction in terms":

> The message my family was getting and giving to me was "He's smart but he's pretty stupid." People never expected what I was. As soon as they met you they had all sorts of expectations about what you performed like in school, and I never measured up to those expectations. The way I came across to people was that if I was in first grade, they figured I should be in third grade; but in school I should have been in kindergarten. So it was very confusing to me. When I was little I had a big vocabulary, was extremely verbal and inquisitive, and asked lots of penetrating questions all the time. Then I'd go to school and fail. I couldn't figure that out.

Not measuring up was reportedly determined in numerous ways. Most people remembered failing to meet traditional academic requirements and being singled out for testing, treatment, and/or special programming. One young woman recollected not being able to do anything in school. She could not read, write, or spell. About the only thing she remembered being able to do correctly was make letters.

> My mother told me I came home one day and said "Mommy, I can't read." Everybody was reading Jack and Jill and I couldn't read it. I said, "Everybody is making fun of me because I can't do it." My parents sent me to some woman who tested me and said that I was learning disabled. So from first grade on we knew I was learning disabled.

Another person remembered reversing letters, reading poorly, and being sent to the back of the room where she was told to read into a tape recorder and then listen to her recordings. Upon hearing this, her parents had her transferred to another school and had her tested.

A young man recalled falling further and further behind despite transferring to other schools to seek improvement. His parents thought he had a vision problem and sent him to a doctor who said, "Your kid doesn't need glasses, he's dyslexic. Get him tested."

Several persons reported that eventually their not measuring up at school became purposeful. As one person remembered, he just wanted out:

> I had problems in school ever since the first grade. I stayed back in the first grade and then again in the sixth grade. The last time I was set back, I ended up dropping out of school halfway through the year. It was kind of an agreement between me and the school district to leave the school. Rather than be called stupid, I started trouble is what it amounted to. Put on the tough act, and that's when I went from there.

Apparently, not measuring up at school could also be attributed to learning disabilities because of one's family history. One person recalled being identified by a teacher who knew that other members of her family had been so labeled previously, and who believed that she probably had the same problems. A similar situation was reported by a college student who had struggled academically and sought the advice of a college official. After discovering that other members of his family had been diagnosed as learning disabled, the official suggested that the student be tested because "if they [family members] all have it, you may also."

At home. Whereas many people pointed to their not measuring up in school as instrumental in being labeled, many reported not measuring up at home. Family members often were pivotal figures in detecting and following up what they perceived as learning problems in their children. Although relatively few parents independently diagnosed their children or sought private diagnosticians, they frequently became heavily involved in their children's difficulties early on, and prodded school professionals to conduct testing and/or remedial services. One young woman related that she was unofficially diagnosed in kindergarten by her mother, who noticed that "something was wrong. I wasn't keeping up as I should, and my mother wanted the school to have me tested. But they refused until I was in third grade." In another situation it was a father who suspected that his daughter had a problem, and prodded the school to take some action:

> My father suspected I had a disability when I was pretty young. He contacted a friend of his who said I was probably dyslexic. So he [my father] used to make me read aloud to him all the time. Then he went to the school district and told them what I would need, like remedial help. They gave me a tutor who made me read aloud.

Some people speculated that their parents' initial involvement had less to do with their own poor academic performance and more to do with their parents' high scholastic expectations. One person noted that "I never thought I had a problem, but my parents did. They began testing me in grade school." Another individual stated: "My parents thought something was wrong and had me tested young because the rest of the family is like a straight-A family." A young woman believed that her problems were due mostly to her own academic indifference and were exaggerated because of her parents' high expectations. She remembered being "just average, pretty typical. I never put in much effort, and just got by. I don't remember it being easy or hard, though I remember being lost in some of the difficult courses. It wasn't me that decided I was having problems, it was my parents."

Several individuals believed that their not measuring up in the family was due not only to high parental achievements and expectations, and sibling abilities, but also to their own self-induced actions. One person admitted he elected to be different:

> When I started first grade, I couldn't learn to read or write as quickly as other kids. I was a very slow reader and I inverted a lot of

letters and words. Spelling was always terrible, and I just avoided reading. I just didn't do it. Our whole family was very academic. My brother and sister both learned to read way before they got to first grade, and I was never anxious to learn. My brother was reading encyclopedias when I couldn't read out loud, and he's younger than I am. My sister was valedictorian and everything. She skipped years in high school. They're all very smart and they used to sit home and read and everything. And I used to go out and play, climb trees, become a derelict. I would never sit home and read.

As noted previously, discord sometimes developed between parents and their children regarding both diagnostic and remedial practices. Furthermore, parents did not always agree with each other on the existence, value, and utility of the label. Apparently, whether or not an individual measured up at home was not self-evident and was a matter of negotiation among family members. Persons who reported that one of their parents did not understand or believe in the learning disabled label remembered being confused about what was really wrong with them and what to do about it. One man recounted the difference in his parents' approaches to him:

My mother understands; but only my mother. My father's a genius, and he could never understand that his kid had a problem. He couldn't deal with it. He loved for me to come down and read, but I couldn't read. I can't read out loud. We'd get into an argument and I'd run upstairs and we wouldn't talk to each other for a week.

My mother kept me together. She knew I was doing my work. She dropped whatever she had to do whenever I had a problem to do. She started reading books on tape and going to the school to help out.

In one situation a person told of being diagnosed as learning disabled through the efforts of his mother but being sent by his father to a psychologist in order to "improve my motivation." Another individual related that his father had never accepted the label but allowed it to be applied until high school. When he saw no improvement in his son's performance, he sent him to a private preparatory high school where the label was seen as a "cop-out." In all but one of these circumstances both parents eventually accepted the label, and, as one person reported in regard to his father's change of heart, "he became more of a friend than a foe."

Avoiding the Label

Not everyone who failed to measure up in school or in their family was officially designated as learning disabled. Whereas each person in the study was eventually diagnosed, many were first identified as having academic problems, but were neither referred for testing nor officially classified until years later. One student, for example, was not officially diagnosed until late in high school after years of academic frustration and parental assistance:

> When I was little, I can always remember feeling stupid and never keeping up with the class and getting in trouble a lot. I would come home and do work and was always frustrated and upset. So she would take me for tutoring. I was never held back, but I was on the verge of it every year. With a lot of tutoring, they pushed me up and put me in slow classes. Somehow I always made it to the next grade. My mother was always behind me, bringing me from one tutor to the next. If it wasn't for her I probably wouldn't have gotten anywhere. Some of my teachers said that I had no interest in school, and that I was only interested in sports. [My mother] used to believe that something was wrong, but she didn't know anything about learning disabilities. I began going to this place where they told me I was dyslexic. I didn't get identified until the end of my junior year [in high school].

Another young woman was not officially classified until she had failed to complete a college English course, although her parents had suspected for years that she had a learning disability. She related that:

> I was beginning to worry that I wouldn't get out of college. I was getting frustrated when my parents approached me and said maybe I should be tested for some kind of disability. They had suspected it for years, but I never knew it. So I went and got tested that summer, and it was discovered that I had a learning disability.

Persons who recounted not fitting in at school and/or at home but who had avoided the official label described several factors that they felt accounted for that situation: (a) parental and professional ignorance, (b) inconsistent professional practices, (c) parental objections to labeling, and (d) individual camouflaging of deficiencies.

Professional and parental ignorance. Many people diagnosed after finishing elementary school felt that they had not measured up to their school situations for years and should have been diagnosed earlier. Some attributed this lag to parental and/or professional ignorance, noting that despite their evident school problems, "no one could figure out what was wrong." One young man remembered failing second grade and having to repeat it, but that

> Through the sixth grade everyone thought I was a normal kid. Then my sixth grade English teacher told me I had to get tutoring or stay back. That summer before seventh grade when I got tutoring was the beginning of my learning disability.

One individual felt somewhat bitter that his disability was not detected sooner, believing that detection might have helped his high-school performance and increased his college options. He indicated that a science teacher "finally figured it out." Had it been detected sooner, he believed, "there would have been a reason for my poor English grades, and I might have gotten into more than one college." Another example of parental and professional ignorance was described by a college student who had only recently found out that he had a learning disability, after living through some extended and traumatic diagnostic experiences:

> It's been about six months that I've known that I could fall under the category of learning disorder. Before that most of my problems in school were attributed to a concussion I had when I was 2 years old. Then I had a deviated septum where my hearing is slightly impaired and they thought that was my problem. [People were] saying, "You fell on your head, you have a deviated septum and don't hear as well as everyone else. Well, we'll straighten this out. We'll bust your nose again." They put two straws in my nose and wrapped cotton around it, and I had that for a week. My hearing didn't improve any and my marks didn't go up drastically. They could come up with everything except that I read very, very slow.

Sometimes parents reportedly assumed that their children had the same problems as other family members or relatives. In some cases they took for granted that their children were learning disabled and had them formally diagnosed. In other situations they assumed that there was little need for classification, accepted the situation as part of their family's life, and did nothing. One young man stated: "My father had an LD, and he suspected that my grandfather did, too. My father didn't do anything about it, because they were kind of used to it."

Inconsistent professional practices. People also attributed their delayed diagnosis to inconsistent professional practices, which had created personal confusion and programmatic upheavals. In one instance a person was classified and reclassified three times before the end of high school:

> I was in resource room until sixth grade. Each year we had to take a test to see if we could go back into the regular class. I took the test in the sixth grade, passed it, and got out of the resource room. Then in tenth grade an English teacher said she thought I was learning disabled. She asked me to take some tests, and afterwards they said I was learning disabled and I should be reclassified. So I was reclassified and sent back to the resource room.

Another person recalled school professionals disagreeing over the advantages and disadvantages of being diagnosed. The school psychologist recommended that the student graduate with Cs and avoid the stigma of the label and special classes. The teacher, principal, and guidance counselor felt that the student would benefit from being classified. As the person remarked: "My parents and I didn't know what to believe."

The existence of diverse professional opinions about learning disabilities was reflected in people's descriptions of their own labeling. Interviewees frequently stated that they were diagnosed because they happened to be at the right place at the right time with the right person. Usually the right person was described as possessing unique qualities or special knowledge. One young woman remembered that "a new counselor, who fortunately knew something about learning disabled students, noticed the discrepancy between what I knew about a course and my performance in the course." Another individual recounted being helped by a teacher who had a son with a learning disability. A third person reported having been identified as a likely learning disabled student by a teacher who had happened to see a television show on learning disabilities the evening before.

Parental objections to the label. Some families did not believe in the learning disability classification. Several persons reported that one or both of their parents believed that they were "lazy, didn't care, or just didn't want to do well." Some parents believed that the label was harmful, as in the following situation:

> When the teachers called me an LD student, my parents didn't understand. They thought the teachers were saying that I was

stupid, or had a retardation problem. My dad was right by saying that they shouldn't break this kid's esteem, that he's not a dumb kid. They said that these tests are wrong. They are saying he's stupid. Just give him some space. I really didn't want to be labeled in junior high on account of my friends, and neither did my father. So we made kind of a stink about it. He said he's definitely not LD. He wasn't doing well because he just didn't want to do well in school. So the testing stopped on a pin and that was that.

In another circumstance, cited earlier, parents initially rejected the label because of warnings from the school psychologist. Eventually they agreed to the label, but only after they were assured that their son could "go for a year classified as being learning disabled and [they could have the diagnosis withdrawn] at the annual review if they wanted to."

Some parents concluded that "something was wrong" with their child, and sought formal verification for their suspicions. However, after receiving an official diagnosis of learning disability, they did not divulge the results to the school or their children. Although most people said that their parents had told them about their early diagnosis after they had again been so diagnosed years later, some parents reportedly never fully revealed the early evaluation results to their children, even after they were formally labeled.

Individuals concluded that their parents had obscured the label because they believed that the classification was potentially stigmatizing and demoralizing, that the condition seemed basically untreatable by the school, and/or that they, the parents, thought they could conduct the required remediation as effectively as the school. One person was not formally diagnosed until college, and understood and accepted her parents' decision to keep her label hidden. She explained: "I can't get my mother to talk comfortably about it [my learning disability]. But I suspect that my parents didn't want me put into separate classes, and didn't want me stigmatized."

Another individual, who was not formally classified as learning disabled until she had failed out of college and been working for several years, remembered her parents' decision with bitterness:

I'm having a very hard time coming to grips with the fact that my mother took me for testing [in elementary school], but she either didn't find out the results or didn't want to find out the results, or couldn't face the results; so I was never informed. I was never told I had a learning disability. Apparently, someone along the way said I had a high IQ, and my mother felt because I had a high IQ I would do fine if I persevered. It could have been a lot more emotionally settling to know what the hell I was persevering for, or why I had to persevere. That's the emotional scarring part, if there is any. What did I have to do this for? And why the hell does it take me so long [to do things]? That's difficult.

Successful camouflaging of problems. Some students stated that they had avoided the label purposely. In order to minimize the stigma of being considered dumb, they gave the appearance of being lazy or unmotivated. They did this by enrolling in less intensive classes, finding ways around their academic weaknesses, manipulating their instructors, and getting in trouble. As one person said, "I just told them [my friends] I was taking these courses because they were easier, and I didn't feel like working hard. My parents just said go ahead and take the easier courses if I thought I would do better." Another young woman stated that during high school she had initially tried to avoid courses that required writing and to "sweet-talk" her teachers into excusing missed assignments. When these strategies failed, she had elected to be placed in "slow-track" courses in order to avoid a formal, stigmatizing label:

> I was never called disabled or retarded or anything in high school. . . . But there were two tracks in high school, and I was put in the slow-track classes that were called BOCES. My friends used to laugh at me, but just joking, and I used to laugh, too. But I was doing my work, and I was doing well. I really don't think I could have done all the regular class stuff. I used to see what kind of work my friends were bringing home and doing and would think, "How could they even do this?" And I had all the nice teachers that were understanding, so I did a lot better. I don't think they taught us anything special, but they went a lot slower. I can't have five different things shoved at me at once, so it was good that they went at a slower pace.

Whereas some people elected to cover up their problems by trying to get along with their teachers and fit in, others diverted attention from their difficulties by acting out. One young man, once an honor student "who got straight As," began to get bad grades after he was asked to read and write more:

> In grade school I was on the honor roll. But in the seventh and eighth grade you start doing more essays, and you're forced to do a

lot more reading. That's when I really noticed [problems], and my grades went down drastically. Then I had some behavior problems. I have to laugh now at the way I handled my problems. I would rather have been thrown out of class or miss school when I knew I may have to read or spell something in front of people.

Escaping the label but feeling disabled. As noted above, many people reported not fitting in at school or at home, temporarily avoiding the *formal* label, but still being treated in both places as if they were learning disabled. Schools could employ various ways of communicating to students that they were deficient without formally labeling them. In previous descriptions people recalled being segregated within their regular class or else sent to a different room. One young woman recalled being sent to the nurse's office with other "special needs" students:

We'd all come in to the regular class in the morning and do a little work. Then we'd end up in the nurse's office. We'd sit in front of the view scanners and play with the little red dot. We lost out but we didn't know that we lost out. I lost out of my first year of school, but we all thought it was great.

Another individual who was viewed as "fooling around and not doing her work" was dismissed from class as a troublemaker:

I had problems in school ever since I started. The first time I stayed back was first grade. I was always pulled out of classrooms away from the other students. I would go into a room with just me or maybe one other student and a teacher. Then I'd go back to class, but halfway through we'd end up leaving. The teachers mainly thought I was horsing around and refusing to do my homework. Then they started sending me to the office, saying, "You don't want to work, so go to the office." In some cases they'd ask me to read, even though they knew I couldn't. When I'd refuse, they'd send me to the office. It got to the point where over half my classes were done in the principal's office.

As described in an earlier section of the chapter, some people had enrolled in "slow-track" courses in order to avoid a formal stigmatizing label of deficiency. And yet, however successfully they may have avoided the formal label, they still received a clear, unofficial message of inferiority, as one person recalled:

I didn't do as well in school as all my friends. I mean, it was visible. I was always put in classes with the nice teacher who understood all the problems that mixed-up, confused people had. I knew I was always behind in my work because they would always say, "Oh, don't worry, you're doing great. Go at your own pace." I never had to read. Maybe that's why I don't do well [in college].

Some people remembered feeling disabled within their families because of the way they were compared with their siblings, and/or because of all the negative attention their relatively poor school performance attracted from other family members. The phrase "relatively poor" was used because numerous students said that their grades weren't "that bad" except when compared with their parents' expectations or their siblings' achievements. Some parents sought only informal assessment and assumed their child's problems were due to factors such as delayed development, emotional difficulties, adolescent laziness or long-standing family characteristics. Frequently parents had concluded that the problem was manageable, elected to avoid any formal labeling, and attempted to manage the problem at home. As will be noted in considerable detail in Chapter 3, such heavy parental involvement was described by many individuals as a mixed blessing. Students mentioned that parental help, although often critical to their academic success, was sometimes overbearing, fractious, and overzealous. As one person remembered, "It [the help] was good, but it made me feel even more stupid." Another individual described "a lot of screaming matches in our house about my schoolwork." Some people reported that their parents had wanted to review and edit every paper they wrote. One young man reported that he had become too reliant upon his parents' help in high school, a situation that undermined his confidence: "I didn't have a strong sense of independence in high school because my parents were always there helping me. It wasn't until college that I realized I could do it on my own."

Seeking the Label

As people entered new, more complex educational environments, they were confronted with tasks they could not handle. For many of the reasons cited earlier, 20 people entered college with no formal diagnosis. Within their first year, however, 16 had been formally classified, all of them because they could not cope with the more demanding academic setting. Student coping and avoidance behaviors, coupled with the interventions of their teachers and parents, likely helped them graduate from high school. These remedies, which were often accompanied by lowered expectations, separate classes and programs, and/or tacit assistance to circumvent students' weaknesses, did not work well in college. In short, to succeed in college people needed the LD label. As one individual ruefully acknowledged: "When I came to college, I just wasn't used to the work. I was used to getting everything handed to me. Now I actually had to do the work and it was scaring me. I realized that I just couldn't do it." A college student, reflecting on his high school years and subsequent label as learning disabled, observed:

> In high school I never had to read. Maybe that's why I don't do well [in college]. Maybe I don't have any learning disabilities, but since I didn't read when I was younger, I don't know how. I was thinking the other day what would have happened if they had sat me down and really explained; and what if I would have done my work?

In college, students found that they could no longer avoid certain academic requirements or manage their instructors as they had done at earlier school levels. One student noted the differences he encountered in college:

> In high school I could just constantly weasel my way around, and I got all Cs. In college I got nailed. I couldn't swing it any more at all. I didn't know how to write an essay, and when you have 200 people and one teacher it's a different story. I wouldn't say the teachers don't care. The teachers care, but there are so many more students that they can't take the emotional time or effort to understand why this kid isn't doing well. They make the assumption that the kid's bright and if he's failing the test, it's because he isn't doing the work.

People also found that working harder didn't always help them in college because the complexity of the work had increased substantially. One young man discovered that

> the college program was very intensive. There was a lot of report writing, field research, and classroom hours. I was asked to write reports which I was never asked to write before. I couldn't do it by just making up time by giving up a job and studying a lot.

As a result of their failure to successfully negotiate their new environment, persons sought answers and relief from their difficulties.

One young man described his search for answers during graduate school:

> When I got to law school, things sort of reversed about 180 degrees, and I had a lot of trouble my first year. It seemed to me the trouble was not so much knowing what was going on or not knowing what to put down, but getting it down on paper; and this went on all through my second year of law school until I went to see the college diagnostician. She finally said yeah, you've got some form of a learning disability. I wasn't surprised, but if someone had told me that I had a learning disability, say, at the end of my sophomore year of college, I'd have said "There's no way," because my grades were very good.

Several persons knew that a formal learning disabilities label would provide some relief from the academic demands of college. One person, who had performed satisfactorily in high school and was never formally labeled, turned to his parents for assistance:

> In college I was dropping out of Spanish and trying to evade Math. I went home to my parents and said, "I cannot pass Spanish in college; it is not possible; and I'll definitely flunk Math." The only way I could get out of this was to get a doctor's note. I wasn't talking learning disabilities. I needed a doctor's note saying that I can't do Math because it was bad for my heart. I got a nice note from a doctor at home, which said I should not have to take Spanish and Math. Later I was formally tested.

Another individual recalled seeking the label when she discovered that she had a disability that entitled her to extra time on the college entrance tests. Interestingly, she also found that her parents had concluded years before that she had a learning disability, but had kept their suspicions to themselves:

> During high school my father showed me how I used to write my name, told me about my reading tutor and the possibility of me being learning disabled. I was shocked. I thought I couldn't do these things because I was stupid. When I took the SATs there was a gigantic difference between my verbal and quantitative parts— something like 350 and 720. I asked my parents if these scores would get me into college, and they said probably, but that my verbal scores were very low because [I] don't read and have a poor vocabulary. I went to my guidance counselor and asked to be tested for a

disability. The school psychologist came in and put me through a whole bunch of tests and said that I had a learning disability. Then I took the SATs again with increased time and scored 490 and 750.

INDIVIDUAL REACTIONS TO THE LABEL

People evidently attached their own meanings to the LD label, as reflected in the diversity of responses they gave when asked how they had reacted to their diagnosis. Some people even reacted strongly to the language applied to their condition, desiring one term over others. For example, one person preferred to be called dyslexic, because "in high school and grammar school learning disabilities meant mental retardation." He noted further: "Dyslexia sounds cooler—you read backwards." Another person favored the learning disability label:

> I use the term learning disabilities. I think there's more to it. I think LD just means you have trouble learning in a conventional way, and you can learn other ways. I just like the term better. Dyslexia is like a dead end, that's it, no hope. It will never change, and you will never change. I don't know, it [LD] just sounds better.

Not only did individuals attach different meanings to the LD label, they also offered definitions and responses that enriched and extended the conceptual, clinical definitions of the professional literature.

Relief

Almost half of the respondents mentioned relief when they described how they had reacted to the LD classification. There appeared to be several different, but often overlapping, descriptions of relief.

From psychological responsibility. Many individuals stated that the label had relieved them of responsibility for their difficulties. For them the label was clearly positive. It provided an official explanation of who they were and why they acted the way they did. One young woman who had been unsuccessful in college and in several jobs related that she had finally found an answer for these failures:

> After several days of testing, the diagnostician said it was obvious I had a learning disability and that she was surprised that it took me

this long to find out. I remember thinking to myself, "There really is a God." I remember leaving her office and being 6 feet off the ground. Finally, I had an answer to why things were the way they were for me. I'll never forget that day.

Another student was relieved to note that he was not to blame for his poor grades, and that despite them he was still officially considered intelligent.

I was so relieved for someone to say that you're bad in math and you're bad in English; that's fine, it's no problem. I knew all along that I was a smart kid. I readily accepted the fact that I was an LD student, and this relieved me of all the previous anxieties [that] I was a bad student. And now I feel even better about being an LD student because I feel like I've lived through something positive. It just made me feel good.

Underscoring their exemption from responsibility, several people presented their problem as a physical/medical phenomenon:

It gave me a new perspective. Before, I knew something was wrong, but I didn't know what it was. At times you tend to doubt yourself, get a little down, think you're stupid. I wasn't sure if it was me or the way I went about my studying. Maybe I didn't pay attention enough in high school or junior high. But it's something in me. It's not something I created through my past. It's in the genes. Realizing that this is what you have to deal with and figure out ways to get around it, like using crutches, to do the things you need to—I think that gave me a little more strength.

Such a perspective was often supported by medical and human service professionals; one person told how this provided some comfort:

After I was diagnosed, it was a weird feeling. I knew there was something wrong with me, and it was good to know that it wasn't my fault and that I wasn't stupid. The doctor explained that there was nothing I could do about it. But it was strange knowing that I had some strange disorder.

For some, the label provided an official verification of their talents. One person acknowledged that such testimony had helped redefine his problem in a more positive way:

I was really relieved to hear the results because they told me I was good at some things, which I knew. I saw that everything I did was either way above average or way below average, and the above average parts encouraged me. I had wondered if my abilities were more bullshit than reality. Now I don't think of it as a disability, but as a specialty. Rather than someone who doesn't have something, I have certain very special, specific aptitudes.

Another individual was also able to redefine his problem and remove some of the generalized stigma that had surrounded him:

It [being labeled] was kind of a relief off my shoulders. It was actually a good thing. It told me something about myself, like maybe I'm not stupid and lazy. I have problems with written expression, and that's how most of the testing is done in school. My manner of conveying information to people is not necessarily my knowledge.

From emotional insecurity. Several people believed that their LD designation not only explained specific problems, but enabled them to develop a new and more positive identity. One person stated: "I've learned to be someone who people can laugh with. I love to be offbeat. I really don't want to be onbeat. I love to be a little bit different."

Another individual emphasized the wisdom that had emerged from his initial emotional insecurities:

I feel that the word *smart* just doesn't mean anything to me, because there are so many ways for people to be smart. I can draw real accurately from life, and people who can't are learning disabled to me. So, I'm very comfortable with it [learning disability] now, but until I was about 25 or so it was a big emotional problem. I think it really limited my professional achievement, limited me from going to school and seeking training when I was in high school.

A young man remarked that the learning disabled diagnosis eventually helped him to see his strengths:

If anything, I've become a stronger person knowing I have a learning disability. I'm more sure of myself now. Before, all I could see was my weaknesses. Now I look at it like, "You're 100% of a person; 20% of you is weakness and the other 80% is strength." I think that being classified as learning disabled showed what my weakness was, which allowed me to look at my strengths and gave me a healthy outlook toward myself. It made me a better person.

From social responsibility. For several people the label was a convenient and respectable way of explaining their problems to the people around them. One man indicated that the label provided not only an explanation for himself but a way of describing his problems to others:

> As these things were presented to me, my area of relief was that I wasn't stupid. The bottom line of it all is feeling inferior, dumb, stupid, any word you want to put on it. I had been going through all the stress and pain, and so much of that was because of not being able to communicate, not knowing what the problem was and how to explain it to people. I didn't know what to tell them before [the diagnosis].

One respondent termed the learning disabled designation "a vote of confidence," because it not only clarified her problems to herself but also enhanced her intellectual and moral standing with others:

> I was labeled learning disabled in the fall of my sophomore year. For me it was a relief because it gave me a reason why things weren't as easy for me as for others, and why I had to work so hard. It was kind of like a pat on the back—good job for working so hard. I came all this way and made it and did very well despite the disability. I felt respected, that people weren't looking at me as a dunce. It was like a vote of confidence.

The label also provided valuable relief from skeptical family members who attributed poor academic performance to laziness. One young man indicated that before he was diagnosed, he had been sent to a psychiatrist who suggested he not be allowed to play baseball until his grades improved. After he was diagnosed, his parents apologized, and their attitude toward him "turned around 100 degrees for the better." Another individual described his parents' attitude before and after his being labeled:

> In elementary school they [parents] would tell me I wasn't trying hard enough and take away my TV time. When I changed schools, I got this counselor who knew something about learning disabilities.

She talked to my teachers and parents and got me tested. After that, when I got a C in a course, my parents would tell me a C isn't so bad. They were very supportive. They'd ask me how I felt about a certain grade, and they were satisfied if I was.

From fear of a worse diagnosis. For some people the learning disabled classification wasn't especially valuing, but it was an improvement over what they had been called previously or had thought of themselves. One young man said: "It [the label] meant that I was dyslexic not stupid; and I'd rather be dyslexic than stupid." Another individual, although skeptical of the new classification, was relieved of a more stigmatizing one:

I was relieved to know that I wasn't retarded, because that's always been in the back of my mind, even now. And then just to know that there was a name for it, and I could do something about it; that it wasn't just me being lazy or that I was slow. Well, I was slow, but there's a difference. But even now I worry that she [the diagnostician] didn't do it right, and that I snuck one by her. That's always in the back of my mind, that I've snuck one by people.

Some skepticism was also expressed by a person who felt some comparative relief, however tenuous it was:

I didn't get diagnosed until the end of 11th grade, so I still had all these problems. For awhile it was like I had this disease. But in a way I was glad. It took a little pressure off me because everyone would say, "You're not stupid, you're dyslexic." At least it was something I had, not just stupidity. Sometimes I'd try to believe them, and I think I was happy.

One young man noted that although the label didn't allow him to redefine himself as smart, it did enable him to think of himself as "not as dumb as I thought." He said: "I used to think most people are smarter than me, but I figure I'm just not book smart. I'm better at hands-on kinds of stuff."

From institutional rejection. The learning disabled classification granted individuals access to social institutions and activities ordinarily closed to people with similar credentials. Many persons expressed relief because the labeling enabled them to obtain the accommodations necessary for them to succeed. This sentiment was expressed by an individual whose accommodations allowed him to graduate from law school:

It was odd that I had to go into law school to find out I had a disability, but I was sick of doing bad in tests. It was a surprise to me, but I'm glad I found out what the problem was. I think I was happy [learning I had a learning disability]. Otherwise I would have thought that I was unsuccessful in law school, because I had a problem basically dealing with the law. There were also advantages to being learning disabled in that I got extra time [on tests] which enabled me to perform better.

A young man saw the label as enabling him to remain in college and as leading the way to a new direction in his life:

I didn't find out until I was 25 years old when I entered college. I went all the way through high school, dropped out in my 10th year, worked in the job market for 7 years until I got frustrated and entered college to try and make a go of it. They discovered I had a learning disability, which helped me stay in school and kind of put me in the right direction.

I always thought I was stupid. It [the label] was a great relief because now I could focus on correcting that and making things better. It restored a lot of self-confidence that I had lost.

positive reaction to label

Following denial. For some individuals psychological relief had followed initial rejection of their diagnosis. These persons distinguished between their initial and later reactions, indicating that their reactions, though severely negative at first, became more positive gradually with the passage of time:

After I found out [about the learning disability] I felt very dumb. I was told my reading was on the fifth-grade level, and I was upset about that. I didn't tell anyone. I knew it wasn't just something very little; it was serious.

After I got to understand it a little better, I realized that this is why I'm not doing as well as other people, and it made me feel a lot better. I could say I have a learning disability, and it wasn't just that they were smarter than me. I wish I could have found out about it a little earlier though.

A young woman explained her difficulty in accepting the label after trying so hard for so long to seem typical:

My reaction was . . . no, I do not have a learning disability. I don't want to hear that or accept it because I had gone through life not knowing this. I've worked so hard and not blamed it on a learning disability. I knew I was different because I worked so hard just to be average; but it was in the file; it was written. I don't know if I ever understood it [the label], but it was nice to know that there was a reason I worked so hard and was just an average student.

Confusion

For many people the learning disabled label was confusing. The designation was amorphous, and it created dissension among parents, teachers, professionals, and labeled individuals who frequently disagreed on the LD designation, what it meant, and what should be done about it. These disparities were captured in the description of a young man who explained his mother's persistent search for answers and solutions to his educational problems:

> I was getting tutored in school and out of school. The best I would ever do would be Cs. It was just really frustrating and I always felt stupid. Some people thought I was pulling the wool over my mother's eyes—over everyone's eyes. One teacher told my mother that she was wasting her time with tutors. She should take me to a psychiatrist. So my mother took me to a psychiatrist, and he couldn't find anything wrong. I think he thought that I was only interested in sports, not in school, so he suggested that I not be allowed to play sports for awhile. So I stopped playing sports and I did just the same [in school] and I was miserable. And my mother told me to go back playing sports. They started doing testing and told my mother that I was dyslexic and should go to this special program.

Ambiguity and controversy. One woman described the controversy that had surrounded her behavior, the conferral of the label, and the selection of the proper program; all of which had left her confused as a child:

> In elementary school they wanted to place me in a BOCES program. My parents didn't understand and asked to test me. So they tested me and found that I had a high IQ; but they said she's not normal and doesn't know how to study. My parents took me to other places to get tested and referred to me as learning disabled. The message I got was: She's smart but she's stupid.

Another respondent also recalled that the label didn't help him understand his situation more clearly or reduce his feelings of general deficiency:

> I understood that I had a learning disability in the second grade. I couldn't read, couldn't write, couldn't do anything in school. I couldn't spell. My mother told me I had a learning problem and that eventually I would learn how to read. But I didn't understand. I just thought I was stupid. I only knew that I was seeing things backwards, and thought that something was wrong in my head.

Many people mentioned that the label was confusing, both to them and to their parents. As one person stated, the diversity of symptoms, etiology, and opinion surrounding the concept had sometimes led to parental skepticism:

> I couldn't say what my learning disability is, really. They said it was a certain type of thinking in areas like math. I also have problems when it comes to reading. They said it would be a disability in some areas but not others, and that it was some kind of chemical thing. My father didn't believe in learning disabilities, which caused some problems in my own mind.

People responded to the ambiguity of their situations differently. One person tried not to worry about it, commenting:

> Here I am; I have dyslexia, but I don't know that much about it. They told me I had it and I didn't know what it was. And she was telling me there are different symptoms, but they just said you have it. But I figured I'm going to have this thing for my whole life, why get upset about it.

Another person reportedly could not help worrying about it:

> You don't understand it [the label]. It drives you almost crazy. I can see someone getting almost violent sometimes. It's a real burden. Why can't I do this? It hurts a lot, and I can see someone becoming very depressed, getting very down on themselves, and not believing in themselves.

Practical consequences. As adults, many people were confused about the label. Several saw advantages to the classification but remained somewhat skeptical about what the designation really meant. A man diagnosed in college was concerned about what the label meant and was confused about how it would affect his eventual employment chances:

It made me feel actually a little better because at last I knew I wasn't stupid like I was led to believe in regular school, years ago. At least I knew that it wasn't my fault that I couldn't spell or anything else, so it made me feel a little better, but I still worried trying to figure it out. Even now I'm kind of afraid because even if I get my degree I'm going to end up going to work, and what happens if I have problems at work, if I misspell reports or something, and they'll say, you have a bachelor's degree because the VA paid for it, but you can't spell. I've been classified as LD, whatever it is; I don't want it, but I've got it. I'm really not afraid to say it, except to an employer. I'd be afraid of losing the job or maybe not even be employed by anyone because of it.

Another person wondered if the classification was really worth all the exasperation and struggle of attending college and aspiring to complex career opportunities:

[After the diagnosis] at first, "Wow, this is great! At least now I know why." But it didn't change nothing. It really didn't. It's helped in the fact that it opened doorways to time extensions. That's a big help, getting books on tape. Not throwing in the towel, that's helped a lot. On the other hand, sometimes I wonder if I'd be better off not knowing, just throwing in the towel and going off and finding another job. College takes a lot of emotional energy out of me and drains me. If I was just working I would have the job and the 40 hours and part time if I wanted it, and then I would be free.

Medical implications. As was noted earlier, numerous respondents attributed their learning problems to medical or neurological factors. Some people believed that their problems stemmed from traumatic childhood events, such as a difficult delivery at birth, a blow to the head, or an early childhood illness. One person referred to his problem as a "chemical thing." Another felt that his problems were inherited, remarking that, "My family doesn't write well or do good in that stuff. My mom doesn't spell well, and she should, she's 50 years old; neither does my sister. So I see it [the disability] in the genes."

Such perceptions were underscored by existing professional definitions and reinforced by the specialists with whom some people consulted. Individuals were consistently told that their problems were physiological deficiencies in thinking. Several persons were referred to physicians and psychiatrists and were given prescription medication for their problems.

For some individuals the medical character of their problem was comforting. For others the implications were perplexing. Several people remembered thinking that there was something wrong with their brain. One person concluded that "something upstairs isn't working, but it's not that I'm nuts or anything." Several people wondered about the changing nature and generalized effects of their condition. One person questioned, for example, whether his condition could change:

> Right now I'm working on some adult testing to really identify if I still have the problem, what it is, and where do I go from here. It's been 20 years [since his first diagnosis], so let's redo it and reclassify and find out what's wrong with me. I want to find out if I'm right being called dyslexic, if I've outgrown it, and it's changed into something else.

Another person thought that learning disabilities may have hidden properties or effects that created personality flaws, noting that "once I got classified, I started wondering if the learning disability caused me to be shy, and stuff, or if it had something to do with it."

A few people were alarmed about the medical ambiguity of their classification. One individual wondered: "Is this a disease? Am I the only one with it?" A woman described her diagnosis as a personal shock that not only connoted a defective brain, but also made her feel responsible for her son's problems:

> I think I'm still reacting [to the label]. I've always known I had a problem, but to actually put a label to it seemed to upset me. After 6 months it still bothers me, and I don't know why. I've coped with it. I got through nursing school, but I guess I feel I have a defective brain. I know I've accomplished a lot. I shouldn't feel guilty and it's no reflection on your intellect. It's been a blow to my self-esteem. You see, I blamed [my learning disability] for the fact that my son's learning disabled. I guess I was surprised that I really was learning disabled.

Another man also worried about passing on his disability to his children:

> My mother and father were both good readers: very bright. I do have a grandfather who I believe may have a learning disability; I'm not really sure. So I don't know if it's passed on. I have no idea. I pray about my daughters, and I watch for it. My daughter is in first

grade now and got straight As, and then got a B in phonics. I just looked at her and said, "Oh, no." But when it [the grade] came back the next time, she got an A. I don't know, I really don't know.

A whole new world. A number of individuals were dismayed by the label, which they felt placed them in a whole new world to which they were unaccustomed. This world entailed new sets of expert and behavioral requirements that made them feel different from others. One person explained this experience:

> In my sophomore year of college it was discovered that I had a learning disability. It was hard deciding what to do. I was advised to leave school for a year and go back and learn how to read right and write and all that. I felt ashamed to tell people at first. I was afraid people would think of me as being different, like handicapped. So when I had to tell my roommate that I was leaving college, I was hysterical; I felt really dumb. I don't know how else to say that but I got over that. I still feel self-conscious about it, but it doesn't bother me as much. I don't go around telling people about it. I've learned to cope with it.

Another person discovered that his learning disability required him to begin what he termed "a whole new life," a process he recalled as particularly difficult:

> In seventh grade I took these tests, and they found out that I had a learning disability. It was kind of a relief because I had failed second grade, and my teachers told my parents that I had something wrong with me. But when the test showed I had a learning disability, I was kind of mad because I had gone through school being taught a certain way, and now I had to start a whole new life. I started over again, and it was really confusing for like 3 years. I was mad and frustrated, and they kept pushing me. It took me 3 years before things began to click over.

One young man described the confusion and emotional trials of discovering that he was really different:

> I found out in sixth grade, and I really didn't know what it was. I felt more different after I was told. I was kind of upset because I thought I was different. I had this problem and no one else did. Before, I just thought I was a slow reader, and I'd eventually get to know how to

read and spell. And then I find out that this problem is why I can't do it.

It took me awhile to get used to realizing I wasn't different. I felt better when I found out my best friend [had] found out he had the same thing, because it wasn't just me who had the problem.

Rejection of Label

Several interviewees were unequivocally negative in attitude toward the label. In some cases they believed that it incorrectly portrayed them. One respondent, for example, believed that the designation connoted a more serious problem than she felt existed. She asserted: "I couldn't tell you what my LD is. It's not that serious, I know that, and I don't really want the label of being an LD student." Another person termed his learning disability label a "crutch," which lowered his and others' expectations of his performance, making Cs and Ds more acceptable.

A young woman acknowledged her problems, but also did not consider them serious enough to warrant her being classified as disabled or being enrolled in an organization for disabled people:

Now I have these newsletters sent to me from the Organization of Disabled Students. Like people in wheelchairs freak me out, get me nervous. I don't see myself as disabled. I look at myself as completely normal. I don't belong in an organization for disabled students. Maybe I'm not as good a reader, but I think a lot of people aren't. I think a lot of people have the same learning disabilities as I do, but aren't tested or aware of it.

Most of those who rejected the label did so because of its stigmatizing consequences. Apparently the response to the problem was felt as worse than the problem itself. Sometimes these responses entailed placement in special classes, which were viewed negatively. One person described the boredom and stigma of his class placement:

All my friends treated me the same, except when I got to middle and high school. Then I knew. I was embarrassed to admit to myself and especially to my friends. At that age peer pressure is probably the strongest thing in the world. They took me out of my regular English classes and I'd work one on one with this lady. I got like As and Bs in there, but we'd do things like color and this was useless to me. I always had a lot of common sense, but they had me in a class with a lot of retarded people. A learning disability is not the same thing as being handicapped in a retarded way.

As noted previously, people also objected to being enrolled in organizations with, or grouped with, people whom they saw as negatively valued. One individual complained that his mother told him that he had to go to the resource room because he had a problem. He did not want to go, however, "because I thought everyone was going to make fun of me. All the retards went there." Another person argued:

> After I found out [the diagnosis] I was surprised. I thought only stupid people had LD. I was confused about what it is and what it meant. I thought that it was more than just being poor in school. I thought it was this whole other stigma, like you're unpopular and have pimples. I thought you don't want to be put in that group.

A young woman rejected the label after experiencing an exclusionary response from another person:

> I didn't want to tell anyone [about my learning disability]. I didn't want anyone to know even in college, because I had told [a college interviewer] that I was dyslexic and the interview totally changed from him talking about me getting into the school as a normal student to him talking about a special program, going every summer, being enrolled in special classes for the handicapped. I decided from then on I wasn't going to tell anyone else.

SUMMARY

The learning disabilities label was described as a setting-specific designation, which was quickly pursued, emphasized, and applied in some schools and families, and ignored or rejected in others.

The label was conferred almost exclusively as a result of poor school performance and could be conferred formally or informally within schools and families. It should also be noted that the LD designation was not always conferred on passive individuals and families. In many instances families and individuals actively pursued or rejected the label, depending upon how they defined it and perceived its effects. In some cases individuals and families rejected the label at one time and pursued or accepted it at another.

A common feature of people's description of their labeling was the recollection of "not measuring up" academically. However, eliciting behaviors traditionally associated with learning disabilities and/or not measuring up to a particular academic setting did not necessarily lead to being formally diagnosed as learning disabled. In fact, many persons reportedly exhibited academic problems associated with learning disabilities that went formally unlabeled for many years. Individuals appeared to become formally labeled when (a) they did not measure up to the academic expectations that others held for them or they held for themselves; and/or (b) their not measuring up was perceived as a problem by themselves or significant others such as teachers or parents.

People's social, familial, and educational circumstances also contributed significantly to their being designated as learning disabled. Most interviewees understood learning disabilities as something within them, and despite having gone undiagnosed for years, they considered their disabilities as "always there," even if undiscovered for a variety of reasons. However, many people in the study would not have been formally labeled unless they had been subjected to certain expectations and/or entered specific settings in which they needed the label to fulfill these expectations. In this sense their labeling could not be divorced from their social, familial, or educational contexts.

Because the label was differentially conferred, it should not be surprising to find that it was also differentially received. For some people the label brought psychological, educational, and social relief; for others it was emotionally upsetting and was rejected as inappropriate. Many described the label as confusing. Several individuals believed that the designation was socially and psychologically helpful at one point in their life but troublesome at another. Many sought the label and accepted it, whereas others tried to escape the designation and rejected it.

Most people expressed confusion and/or relief about the learning disabilities designation. Even those who had sought and/or relied on the classification for assistance did not often understand it. In addition, many were troubled by some of the label's consequences. The use and value of the label itself, for example, frequently were issues of debate and dissension among those around the person. Labeled people themselves raised questions about the value of the label, especially how it would affect their social and employment prospects. For some the diagnosis introduced the specter of medical and genetic dysfunctions that might be passed on to children. As McGuinness (1986) concluded, a designation of learning disabled created anxieties and sometimes led to more serious problems for both families and individuals so labeled:

The school's appropriation of clinical terminology has resulted in an
enormous population of parents who believe that their children have
some irredeemable congenital or pathological disorder. In fact,
based on some follow-up research on learning disabled children, it
appears that this kind of irresponsible labeling can produce symptoms much worse than those that led to the diagnosis in the first
place. Labeling of any kind is often undesirable, but in the absence
of pathology . . . is especially pernicious. (p. 3)

Finally, the label placed people into what they described as the
whole new world of expert definitions, procedures, and prescriptions.
Depending upon their age, this could include being placed in special
classes or schools, being socialized to affiliate with other learning
disabled and/or disabled students, and being advised to introduce
themselves to teachers and/or employers as learning disabled.

Whereas many persons felt confused by the label, some reported
confusion, disorganization, and frustration without it. In the latter
cases, people's confusion was apparently mitigated somewhat by what
they perceived as the more coherent state of professional prescription,
protection, and control that surrounded their learning disabled designation. Many accepted the diagnosis readily and some even sought it
out because, following a history of school failures, individuals considered themselves stupid. And as one person expressed it, "Being learning disabled was better than being stupid." Thus the label provided
many people with a legitimate, more valued interpretation of their
problems and afforded them institutional help in achieving their academic and social goals.

In discussing the diagnoses of blindness and physical illness re-
spectively, Scott (1969) and Balint (1972) noted that with a formal
diagnosis patients moved from the unorganized stage of illness/defi-
ciency into one involving order, prescribed roles, and courses of action. Balint observed that whether or not one agrees with that definition, "to know 'what I have' is a key turning point in the illness
experience" (p. 76).

Based upon the circumstances and responses of those labeled,
there is genuine doubt as to how much real clarity, order, and effective
prescriptive action emerged from people's diagnosis. There is little
doubt, however, that the diagnosis represented a central organizing
point in people's psychological, educational, familial, and social experiences.

3

Managing School and College

Students with learning disabilities employed many formal and informal techniques in order to succeed academically. Under the Rehabilitation Act of 1973 and the Education for All Handicapped Children Act of 1975 (P.L. 94-142), individuals were entitled to many formal accommodations designed to minimize instructional, social, and environmental barriers and to equalize opportunities for social, academic, and vocational success. Specific formal accommodations included extended time for examinations and course assignments; tutoring and proofreading services; use of tape recorders in class; textbooks on tape; and reduced course loads. These accommodations were frequently used in college, but rarely employed in elementary or high schools, where special class placements served as the major formal accommodation.

Students also used *informal* accommodations to manage the academic requirements of school and college. Informal accommodations included the manipulation of instructors and the use of parental and peer assistance. Although clearly covert, these strategies were as critical to student success in schools and college as formal accommodations.

FORMAL ACCOMMODATIONS

Using Accommodations in Elementary and High School

Within elementary and high schools the most prevalent way of assisting persons with learning disabilities was the special class placement. In "pull-out programs," students were removed from regular classes and placed in separate classes. These placements included students who had been formally designated as intellectually and academically deficient. In most cases students with learning disabilities attended separate classes for a portion of the school day, returning to regular classrooms (often, however, to slow track classes) for the remainder of the day.

Some students reported that they had been helped by special class placements, because teachers had given them the individualized, extra help they needed to complete their homework, to read, write, and organize their written assignments better, and to carry out special class projects. Most students, however, disliked special class placements. As noted in chapters 2 and 4, these placements were cited as the most stigmatizing aspects of people's school years. Although a few students who were not formally diagnosed were enrolled in special classes, most were enrolled in slow track classes or negotiated their way through regular classes using informal accommodations. Informal accommodations are described later in this chapter.

In college, students enrolled in the same classes as their peers, and the accommodations they received were designed to assist them to remain in those classes and succeed academically. However, during elementary and secondary school few students received formal accommodations that allowed them to remain in regular classes. Only one person reported using a textbook on audio tape to assist with his reading assignments. The same individual recalled taking a few tests orally in high school. In both cases these accommodations were suggested by a father who worked as a counselor for people with visual disabilities, and were used only sparingly in the student's latter years of high school. Two other students used tape recorders in class. Both gave the idea up, however, because the practice made them appear too different to other students. In each of these cases the accommodations were isolated, improvised occurrences that were suggested by parents or outside professionals, and were neither suggested nor encouraged by school personnel.

Using Accommodations in College

Untimed tests and time extensions. The most frequently cited formal accommodation was the untimed exam. People described this as the most helpful, "the biggie," because it neutralized slow reading habits, comprehension difficulties, and written composition. As one student noted, "It took the pressure off so that I didn't freeze up worrying about the time."

Virtually all of the students used this accommodation and attested to its helpfulness. Many, however, complained that test-taking distractions were significant problems. They were unable to take full advantage of a time extension unless provided a quiet location in which to take the test. Finding a separate room was often more difficult to achieve because of students' reluctance to ask such assistance, the difficulty in finding an available location, and the frequent lack of instructors' willingness to make these arrangements.

People did not favor time extensions for class assignments as much as they did for exams. Many students bemoaned the shortage of time to complete their assignments, and needed to take incompletes at the end of semesters or finish their work during semester breaks or summer recess. Other individuals, however, avoided taking incompletes or even requesting time extensions to finish assignments. As one person related, "Time extensions just put you behind even further."

Tutors and proofreaders. Students with learning disabilities were eligible for free tutoring; many took advantage of the opportunity. They used tutors for problem courses or problem course requirements, such as writing papers. As one individual stated, sometimes tutors became indispensable:

> I needed a tutor to get through my classes. That's all I needed. If it weren't for [my tutor] I wouldn't have gotten through. She rewrote my English papers. I mean, I put my thoughts down, but you couldn't read it; it made no sense; it was really choppy, she was like my editor. If I had to write a paper for my poetry class, she would read the poem and we would go over the poem and do the paper together.

The overall reviews on tutors were mixed. Some students felt that tutors were not especially helpful, because they were paid very little and did not often share the same major or classes. Tutors were sometimes viewed as indifferent to, and unaware of, the problems confronting individuals with learning disabilities. One individual explained, "Tutors didn't help. They don't know what's really happening in class, or what the teacher expects. Friends are more invested, much better; they know what's expected."

In most cases persons who had benefited from tutoring did so because they had very specific ideas about what services they wanted from tutors, and because they carefully managed their tutors. One young woman described her techniques as follows:

> I hire a lot of tutors; that's probably my primary thing. I find foreign graduate students who aren't allowed to work in the U.S. and pay them. I tell them to pretend they're giving me a lecture, and I get the material I need repeated that way. Or I'll pick a problem that I'm having trouble with, and I ask them to help me solve it. That's

probably the best technique. It really makes a difference having a good tutor.

Many people felt that they needed tutorial assistance but rejected the idea of tutors. Some did so for reasons cited earlier, and some felt very stigmatized if they used tutors to the extent that they actually needed them. One student reported that she used tutors in two subjects and needed them in two others. However, she felt stupid for using so many tutors and was afraid her friends would find out.

To obtain assistance, people relied heavily on their friends instead of tutors. In fact, nearly all of the people studied revealed a consistent and pervasive dependence on the people around them for assistance. Students with learning disabilities described spouses, parents, friends, lovers and/or teachers as critical determinants of their academic success or failure. People's reliance on their friends is discussed in more detail later in the chapter, in the section on informal accommodations.

Textbooks on tape. About a third of the individuals interviewed mentioned taped texts as helpful. People used recorded texts in various ways. Some read along with the tape; others only listened. Some people could not use the taped texts to assimilate detailed technical information, whereas others saw taped texts as a time-saving, invaluble resource for all of their courses:

> I made an effort to get as many books as possible on tape—textbooks, classics, novels. I always bought the books and read along, and I would say it at least doubled my reading speed and improved my concentration. It was really wonderful to take a literature course and sit down and read it in 3 hours and be done. I had a class at 11:00, so I'd get up at 7:00 and read until 10:30 and know the book. It would be so fresh and crackling in my mind that I could recite it. That really made all the difference.

Textbooks on tape also served as an important supplement to more conventional studying and the use of tutors. As one young woman described it:

> I use books on tape. You can get a lot of the engineering texts on tape. I can listen really quickly to books on tape, but there's something about the technical material that requires you to go back over and over and over it. Books on tape really aren't suited for that. It's all right if I'm sort of skimming; I put the tape on high and let the

words wash over me. Then when I go back and read it, it's familiar, so it's easier to read.

One individual reported that recorded texts not only helped him with his course work, but also had given him an appreciation for reading that he had never had or understood in others:

We had to read a paperback for one of my classes, and to this day it's one book I would never forget. It was the first tape I ever got from the Recording for the Blind, and I read along with it. I was watching the words as I was listening to the tape, and it was the first time I ever read a book and understood it cover to cover; and I was 27 years old. I still remember it because I was able to understand why people liked reading books. I hate books because I don't understand them. They make no sense. I'd rather watch TV. But I got more out of that one book than from anything I think I've ever done.

Some people found taped texts a nuisance. Many books were not available on tape. Others were difficult to obtain. Many students complained that the texts had to be ordered months in advance because they took so long to arrive. Several persons also reported that some technical texts were unnecessarily time-consuming for persons with vision, because they described graphic, tabular, and photographic materials in such detail.

I really listened to them [tapes] for a couple of chapters and then stopped because they're really for somebody who is blind. If the book has graphs and pictures, the people reading go off and start describing what's in the picture and graph. That takes a lot of time. I found that I could read it myself and go quicker than the tapes.

Tape-recorded classes. About one fourth of the students interviewed reported that at one time or another they tape-recorded their classes. Some people recorded courses that were particularly troublesome, whereas others taped only specific lectures. Most of those who recorded their classes rarely if ever listened to the tapes. As one young man noted: "Who has time both to go to class and to relisten to all the lectures?" Another person remarked that it would be nice to have written notes on all the class lectures, but that she didn't have the time or money to transcribe all the taped material. Apparently, many students taped classes as much for psychological as for academic reasons.

One person noted: "I tape my classes but rarely play back the tapes. It calms me down and I get more out of class. In case I miss something, I know it's there, like a crutch."

Not only were tapes time-consuming to listen to and difficult to have transcribed, they were also seen by some as intrusive and stigmatizing in class. One individual refused to use a tape recorder even though she needed it:

> The tape recorder would probably help, but I would be too embarrassed to bring my recorder to class every day. A girl in summer school used one, and the recorder would stop and the whole class would have to wait for her to change the tape. So I've never done that even though I can't get all the professor's notes down, and when I look at my notes they look like little fragments.

Reduced course loads. Numerous individuals stated that they took reduced course loads because they required more time than other students to complete the assignments and papers. They were allowed to do this and retain their status as full-time students because of their designation as learning disabled. Retaining full-time student status was very important for receiving financial assistance.

Some people reported that 9 or 12 credits was their limit per semester, and they never registered for more than that. Other students explained that they usually signed up for a full 15-credit load and retained those credits, if possible. If a course became too demanding, however, they dropped it altogether until the start of another semester or until the next summer. Instead of dropping demanding courses, some told their professors that they were unable to finish the course requirements and requested incompletes. Because of their disability, they were allowed to take incompletes despite instructors' policy against this practice. Incompletes were erased when the student had completed the course requirements and received a final grade.

Several students used channels to eliminate troublesome courses altogether. To do this they requested exemptions from particular courses that required skills in which they were deficient. If their advisor refused, they appealed. After a formal appeals process, college officials granted exemptions in all of the reported situations.

Special colleges. In most instances people with diagnosed learning disabilities comprised a distinct minority of their college's student body. Upon admission to the college, or upon identification, they were typically referred to an office of student services or an academic support unit, where they were acquainted with the accommodations available to them. Academic support staff provided assistance and support in obtaining accommodations from individual professors. Under this kind of system students were responsible for approaching their professors, explaining their problem, arranging for accommodations, and seeking tutorial assistance from the academic support unit.

About 20% of the students in the study had attended special colleges that actively recruited students with learning disabilities and provided more intensive services than those found at more traditional colleges. At these special colleges students with learning disabilities could comprise anywhere from 100% to 40% of the college's student body, thereby constituting a greater proportion of the student body than would occur at typical colleges.

At most special schools persons with learning disabilities attended classes with the other students, but also had separate activities and classes in which they were expected to participate. At one college, for example, people with learning disabilities attended summer school, where they learned writing and organizational skills. Following the summer experience, they were assigned a faculty member who, during the regular academic year, served as a liaison with their teachers and as a resource person. At some schools students with learning disabilities were expected to attend a special study room at least 9 hours per week, during which time they would review course material with a resource person or other students and use tape recordings of their texts, which were on reserve for them. Individuals were also allowed to take the tests in their advisor's office, where they were given extra time if they needed it.

Schools with more intensive programming expected persons with learning disabilities to report to a designated counselor for tutoring and/or advising, to join group meetings consisting of other students with learning disabilities, and, if deemed necessary, to take a one- or two-semester sequence of noncredit preparatory courses. At some colleges the preceding activities were designed only for students with learning disabilities, whereas at other schools they were attended by individuals designated to be "academically in need."

Reactions to special colleges were mixed. Some students described the experience as being helpful in "getting them into the college swing of things" and in serving as avenues of transfer to "real" colleges. Others objected to aspects of the colleges as different, separatist, and "glorified high schools." One young man felt that the school he attended gave him self-confidence but believed that the school was

very stigmatizing because of the paucity of work it required, the type
of students it attracted, and its general reputation:

> They weren't colleges. They were learning disabled schools. To me
> they were nothing. I wanted to go to a college. I didn't like the idea
> that people around me were stupid, and no one cared about
> school. I could sit there and not read a book and get a C on a test. I
> never could do that before. I used to have to know something
> about the subject. The only classes I took notes in were my history
> and English classes. There were two history classes I didn't do a
> damn thing [in] and got Bs and Cs. I got a 3.0 my last semester and
> didn't do a damn thing except for English. It was high school. I just
> went in and took a test—all untimed. I figured I'd take advantage of
> what I could get. [The college] did help me realize that I could do it,
> but I wanted to go to a school that had a name.

Several individuals objected to the lack of privacy that enrollment
in such schools entailed. One student, who "just wanted to be like
everyone else," complained about the special study skills center attended only by students with learning disabilities. On the other hand,
at schools which had an "open" study skills center, students reported
regular attendance if "a lot of the regular students used it."

Another facet of the privacy issue was described by a person who
enrolled in a special college but did not wish to be formally identified
as learning disabled and did not reveal her label on her application.
She was upset to be contacted by the school's special counselor for
learning disabled students. She became further irritated to learn that
the counselor routinely reviewed the academic records of all incoming
students for "signs of learning disabilities."

Some individuals expressed displeasure with the noncredit ar-
rangement that they reportedly discovered only after their enrollment.
This practice, which consisted of enrolling students in noncredit
courses (for the same tuition costs as credit courses) in order to bring
them up to college level proficiency, was characterized by some
students as "a repeat of high school." One student, who had been
identified as learning disabled in elementary school but who had
received no high-school accommodations, was upset to discover that
she had to take some noncredit coursework:

> When I got here the [academic] counselor told me she was going to
> put me in all noncredit [courses]. She said that I would have to go to
> this reading skills class in the morning, and take noncredit math and

English and drop psychology and accounting. I didn't know what she was talking about and was really upset. I talked to the [learning disability specialist], and we decided that I could keep my regular English class and accounting but had to drop psychology and take the noncredit math.

Special college staff and programs. At all of the colleges studied, a designated counselor or staff specialist was available to students with learning disabilities. These professionals performed a variety of duties including testing, counseling, tutoring, and advising; informing students of classroom accommodations; advocating for them with faculty, and talking with family members. Most students saw these professionals as very important to their success. They were viewed as learning experts who could explain their academic problems, offer emotional support and practical advice, legitimate student needs for assistance with faculty, and prescribe a set of formal remedial procedures. As one young woman succinctly recalled: "My learning disabilities specialist made me understand what a learning disability was." Such instruction included specific ways of understanding and presenting one's disability, and of eliciting the cooperation of one's instructors:

The specialist gave me a sheet with all of the accommodations I needed on it. I was supposed to hand it to my class instructor on the first day of class and explain that I'm learning disabled. They circle the accommodations which apply to their class, though technically I'm eligible for all of the accommodations listed on the sheet. I also give them a sheet which describes more about learning disabilities and accommodations. After they read it, they are supposed to sign it. Their signature means they know I'm learning disabled, and they agree to give me these special things.

Another person reported that a specialist helped him deal with many long-standing emotions and clarify many long-standing questions:

[The specialist] made me feel very, very special—unique, and that's very important. They didn't present [the disability] as a handicap but as something rare and unique. They concentrated a great deal on my achievements, and I think their surprise made me feel even more special. They could have talked only about the negativism, and it would have been worse. It would have driven me into inse-

curity. It was almost that I enjoyed spending time with them, so I
think they deserve a great deal of credit. I also saw a film on the
learning disabled adult shown by [the specialist]. It got into a lot of
the dynamics, the heartbreak and sorrow of a person who is suffer-
ing from an unseen handicap. And I remember crying. I wish I had
seen the film when I was younger . . . because so much of the pain
was not being able to communicate, not knowing what the problem
was and how to explain it to people.

Another person praised the learning disabilities specialist as
"wonderful," because she was informative and reassuring, clarifying
test results and offering moral support and practical advice:

She's one of the people who kept me in school. After being tested, I
got a big report about what it all meant. It was all very vague—
statistics and analyzations, and numbers I couldn't understand. It
said I could get so-called help, but I didn't know what kind of help.
I was just happy someone was standing behind me, saying go ahead,
like we're on your side now. I think I needed someone to just pick
me up and stand behind me.

A young man reported that the strengths he doubted that he had
were clearly illustrated for him by the learning disabilities professional:

After she [the learning disabilities specialist] tested me, I was relieved. When she showed me my scores, there was this empty space
in the middle of the scores. Everything I did was either way above
average or way below average. It meant that my verbal skills were
good. My recall in certain types of things was good, so that was
encouraging. I was always dealing only with my problems, and I
wondered if my abilities were more bullshit than realities.

Specialized staff were also considered important because they
had institutional power. Besides formally defining which people were
"officially disabled" and providing specific remedies, specialists had
the institutional authority to mandate faculty compliance. A law school
student recounted the power of the learning disabilities label to obtain
classroom accommodations:

Because she [the specialist] diagnosed me as having a learning
disability, I was allowed more time on tests, and that's very unusual.

Most law schools are very strict on allowing exceptions, because they fear that it will cause an uproar if one student is found out to have an advantage. Law school is very competitive. And as far as the other students were concerned, I kept it quiet. The associate dean requested that I do that, and I think he was correct. Some people would automatically be suspicious.

Faced with intransigent instructors, one student used the special services office to threaten faculty into compliance:

A lot of my professors looked at me and said "You don't look disabled," because I look normal and can speak properly. They didn't believe me, and you're not going to sit there and argue with the teacher. I made them accept it by throwing out names. I said, "If I can't get these things, I'll have to call [the office of] student services and ask them to discuss it with you." Then they got all nervous and said that we could work it out.

Another student described his experiences before and after obtaining the help of the specialist:

I had failed chemistry, and I asked the chemistry professor what I could do to get a better grade. And he said that I should listen to his tape. Well, I listened to it, and there was just no way I could do it. And I asked him if I could get some help from someone, do some extra credit, do something to get my grades up. And he said no. If I was able to punch his lights out, I would have. I took it really hard. I took it personally because that was one of the courses I was really having problems with. After I got tested, [the specialist] got a reader for me and got me a proofreader. I did a lot better. I learned from that. People don't take things from what you say. You have to have it in writing. You can't talk with teachers without having somebody behind you.

Several interviewees based their choice of college on whether there were specialized staff and programs available for them. One individual remarked that she had only visited one college "because I was told that they had programs for learning disabled people, which could help me." She also noted that the specialized program helped her because "I know other people are having problems too. It makes me feel better—not good—but makes you feel that you're not alone."

One person who had transferred from another college recalled the difference in the services she received when there was a specialized program:

> After I was tested, I went back to school and approached a lot of teachers, and told them what I needed. But I was getting nowhere. It was like a dead end there. No one was willing to help you out there. They were talking about getting a system, but it was going to take another year or two. So I decided to transfer to [another college] because they had a support system, and I'd be working with [a specialist], and if I had any trouble she would intervene for me. Here I just showed my professors the letter that [the specialist] had given me. They were all super, saying, "If you need any help, just come see me." Nobody gave me any problems at all.

MINIMIZING AND AVOIDING FORMAL ACCOMMODATIONS

Despite their desire for special considerations, many students applying to college viewed specialized staff and programs with a critical eye. On one hand they sought evidence of a program presence, but on the other hand they desired a certain degree of anonymity. One person described the balance she sought:

> One school I applied to insisted that I enroll in a very structured summer program for learning disabled students. That was too much—overdoing it a little. At another school I went to their handicapped program office, this little cubicle; and they didn't seem to know what a learning disability was. So that was not a plus for the school. In fact, it was a triple minus that they didn't have anything. At this school I met the person who ran the program, and she introduced me to a student with a learning disability. They had a program I liked.

One interviewee remarked that the specialist's suggestions were "prepackaged" and did not conform to his way of doing things. When he had questioned her suggestions, he was told that "he was on his own," and reportedly did not receive much help from her. Several individuals did not like the specialized program because of the stigma they associated with it. One person did not like being grouped with disabled people in general, noting that during a special orientation session for disabled students, she was uncomfortable being grouped with people in wheelchairs. Another individual objected to being singled out from her peers for any reason.

Several students felt that specialized programs were greatly overrated. They felt that resistant faculty could still undercut recommended accommodations too easily. Students recounted how some instructors had brushed aside their initial requests for accommodations by saying they should not worry about that until a need for extra assistance became evident later in the semester. Some students recalled being discouraged because they had to provide faculty with long, detailed explanations of their problems. One person described an instructor who had rejected his request for accommodations, arguing that spelling and punctuation were not important enough in his class to warrant extra time. Another student remembered a professor giving him extra time, but standing over him for practically the entire duration and asking him repeatedly when he would be finished.

The vast majority of students used combinations of formal accommodations depending on the class situations they encountered. About one third, however, avoided all or some accommodations. A few persons considered all accommodations as charity. One individual stated: "I don't take handouts. I get to know my teachers and iron out any problems I'm having with them individually." Another student considered accommodations "just an excuse for being lazy," which he "only used once, and that was only to get extra time." Some people rejected certain accommodations because of the embarrassment they experienced. A few reportedly avoided tape recorders altogether. And one person would not use a tutor under any conditions, noting that "when I do papers, I never let anyone read them. I'm very sensitive about that." This student did say, however, that occasionally he asked a trusted friend to proofread his papers.

In order to accomplish their educational goals "by themselves, and without the hassles of extra help," several students used accommodations minimally. One person who used time extensions throughout law school took the bar exam without accommodations, "just to show myself I could do it." Another student who had avoided test-taking accommodations continued the practice "to avoid the hassles and to feel like everyone else, even though I could kick myself afterwards, when I have to rush through the test and know I could have had an A."

According to some, instructors and non-LD students resented accommodations. One person reported avoiding potential hostility and embarrassment by "only going (to school) part-time and gaining extra time that way." Several individuals warned that faculty reactions could be unpredictable, and that the subject of accommodations had to be introduced cautiously. One individual believed that some of his professors felt "threatened" by a tape recorder because they feared students selling their notes to colleagues who were not in class.

Students also found that instructors misunderstood the reasons why students needed the extra help. Several students reported that requesting or receiving accommodations backfired, creating a "negative self-fulfilling prophecy":

> The teacher will find out who is an LD student and think he's stupid. This has definitely happened to me. Once you approach a teacher saying you're an LD student, they will come closer to you, they speak slower, and it's funny. I just go "Oh, Jesus." So now if I think I'm in danger of that happening, I don't even get any accommodations signed. I'd rather not have the teacher think I'm that way. Because I know in one of my classes, I walked in there with an A average, and I got a D on the final. And I told him right before the final that I was an LD student. And I know my exam was graded differently. I could see it with my own eyes that he treated me 100% differently.

INFORMAL ACCOMMODATIVE STRATEGIES

Formal accommodations were mandated by law and were the right of individuals designated as learning disabled. Whereas people depended on formal accommodations to succeed in school, informal arrangements were viewed as equally crucial to their success. Informal accommodations were unofficial improvisations developed by students to help them complete their academic work and to minimize the stigma of needing extra help. Two of the most frequently mentioned informal strategies were instructor management, and family and peer assistance.

Managing and Manipulating Instructors

Because of the high schools' reliance on special class placements, high school students had less accommodative flexibility than college students. In order to avoid such placements, people attempted to manipulate their instructors and avoid detection as inferior students. One young woman endured being considered lazy in high school in order to avoid the chance of being discovered as an inferior student:

> I always used to get out of the courses that required a lot of reading. I always found a way to sweet talk my teachers and get out of things. There were two tracks in high school, and I was put in the slow-track classes that were called BOCES. My friends used to laugh at me, but just joking, and I used to laugh, too. But I was doing my work, and I was doing well. I really don't think I could have done all the regular class stuff. I used to see what kind of work my friends were bringing home and doing and would think, "How could they even do this?" And I had all the nice teachers that were understanding, so I did a lot better. I don't think they taught us anything special, but they went a lot slower. I can't have five different things shoved at me at once, so it was good that they went at a slower pace.

Several students described how they manipulated their teachers by "getting through on a smile," as a young man put it. Another person stated:

> When you're younger you learn to work your way around things. In high school teachers tend not to go by such strict numbers, especially when you're younger. It's not like, bing, bing, numbers turn out to give you a certain designated grade, like it is in college. So you can really learn to work with people. I was a bad student, but at the same time you learn to work your way around.

One young man explained that he had circumvented his weaknesses and managed to fit in within regular classes, although he remembered never having read a textbook. He took detailed class notes, listened attentively and participated actively in class, and studied diligently for tests:

> I tried to review my notes, but they were awfully chaotic, so I basically relied on what I heard in class. I would do the written homework and get mediocre grades because I wasn't coherent. Most of the tests were multiple choice and came from class notes, so I'd get good grades on the exams. So they'd figure I did the homework and I'd get good grades. Every so often I'd get an essay question, and I'd hand in an incoherent test. The teacher would usually call me up and ask me what I meant by this passage, and if I could explain it I'd get an A, if not I'd get a D. Usually I could explain it.
>
> Mostly I didn't really have to hear it more than twice and I'd get it. I participated during the questions and answers, the teachers

always liked me, and we got along pretty well; that was certainly on my side.

In college students had to perform in the same academic arena as their peers. Though entitled to certain accommodations, students soon learned that the cooperation of the professor greatly enhanced the academic and social value of the accommodation. Some instructors would resist modifying their classroom procedures, giving students only partial accommodations or persuading them to postpone receiving any special considerations until they "showed that they really needed them."

Some professors reportedly were indiscreet and caused some students with learning disabilities considerable embarrassment. One faculty member complained in the presence of other students about having to grant accommodations to a particular individual. Another instructor, apparently trying to be helpful, introduced a student to the class as a "courageous student with a learning disability" who would be receiving special assistance. Out of an awareness of the potential for such humiliating experiences, most students learned "to read their instructors" before requesting accommodations.

Most persons did not tell their instructors about their learning disability or request any accommodations on the first day of classes. As one student stated:

> Many teachers don't know what I'm talking about when I tell them. Some can even be abusive. So I get to know my teachers. Every teacher I have knows my name when I see them on campus. I talk with them and express an interest in their course.

In fact, students were quite circumspect in their approaches to instructors, often waiting until they had a "feel" for the kind of person he or she was before requesting accommodations. Some students had specific signs they looked for in their instructors:

> I go the first day and look them over and make some guesses about them. If they announce office hours, I'll go after class and ask if I can talk to them. People who announce office hours are usually pretty reasonable people. They'll talk to you, make time for you, and don't mind sitting in their office when no student comes. If they say I'm always in my office, you can come find me, it sets off bells and whistles, I say, O.K., this is a person who really doesn't want to take time out with a student who is going to give him some

trouble. Then I might wait until the first homework assignment has been turned in and I do remarkably well. And then I'll go and say I need to tell you about this problem I have. So, it doesn't always work that way, but I sort of have a system for doing this.

Another student also tied his approach to certain impressions he formed of a person:

So now I go in and I look at the teacher. It's very important to go to the first two classes because the teacher really gives out a lot of information about himself the first two days. I try to read them. If a person seems open-minded I will approach them. What I tend to find is that older people still think that people should be writing with their right hand; if you write backwards, you're not a good student, but kind of retarded. A lot of these teachers have been doing research for years and are closed-minded, and I won't approach them. I'll take what I can from them and just go.

Not all students could delay or avoid telling instructors about their disability. They admitted that telling their professors was difficult because of the possibility of being misunderstood, embarrassed, and/or refused. However, they believed that they had little choice. As one person said: "It's hard to be seen as different, but it's fatal if I don't tell them or wait too long."

Some people adopted a consistent pattern of showing their professors, on the first day of class, a form developed by the college's special services office, which identified them as learning disabled and provided information about the requested accommodations. This strategy was applied to all of their classes regardless of the instructor's demeanor. It was the approach most widely recommended by the college counselors and staff specialists who advised students on these matters. As was noted earlier, however, most students resisted such blanket strategies and informed instructors on a selective, "as needed" basis.

Students who did divulge their learning disabilities and request accommodations on the first day of class pointed to specific reasons for doing so. One individual who had experienced problems with a previous instructor stated: "I go up to each teacher right away; or else later in the year when you're having trouble, they'll ask you 'Why you didn't come up sooner?'"

A young woman who consistently divulged her learning disabilities to her teachers on the first day of class had done so because she believed it had helped instructors remember her and had enabled her to make a positive first impression:

> I hand the academic accommodations sheet to my teachers on the first day and introduce myself as learning disabled. In this way teachers know my name, and I can go back after a test and go over it. Teachers will give you the benefit of the doubt if you're border-line and show that you are trying.

Whether they told their instructors or not, the vast majority of persons emphasized the importance of getting to know their instructors and making sure that their instructors knew them. Students consistently mentioned that they made special efforts to "sit down with their teachers, and let them know you're interested and trying hard." Only two people used terms like "brown-nosing" and "buttering up," but many strongly implied the need to ingratiate themselves with their teachers. This meant sitting in front of the class, both to show interest and reduce distractions. It meant being on time for, and rarely missing, class. It meant seeking the instructor out to discuss topics and raise questions, asking questions and being informed and prepared in class, and letting the instructor know of the learning disability and desired accommodations in terms the professor could understand. Despite their right to accommodations, most students saw themselves as dependent on their professor's good will for the qualitative aspects of accommodations. That is, they depended on instructors' help and friendship in order to perform well academically, retain a positive emotional outlook, and maintain a solid social standing with peers.

Whereas students wanted to avoid an adversarial relationship with their professors, they were nonetheless aware of their rights as disabled students and what their options were if they did not obtain the accommodations they needed. Not receiving necessary accommodations was often more deleterious to them than incurring the wrath of their instructors. Thus most people were assertive and persistent when they had to be. One individual who had nearly flunked out of college related:

> Some of my teachers were good about it, but some weren't happy with it and looked at it as extra work they'd have to do. So a lot of time I didn't speak up in the beginning, and I probably could have been getting more help. And I just let the teachers talk to me and they'd say, "I don't think you need this," and I'd just let it go. Sometimes maybe I felt like I really didn't deserve the extra help.

Now I'm telling myself I have to go out and do it myself; I can't let anyone talk me out of it; that's what's coming to me. I have it legally. Like with that summer school teacher who gave me a problem, I guess I just stood up for myself more.

Reduced course loads were also used to make people's education as easy as possible and to circumvent troublesome instructors and courses, even required ones. Several individuals openly admitted that they were looking for the easiest courses they could find, so as to maximize their academic average and class standing. They routinely signed up for 15 credits, fully intending to drop the one or two most difficult courses. In this way they were able to test the requirements of individual courses, and the difficulty and flexibility of specific professors, without jeopardizing their full-time status. In some cases students would then avoid such courses altogether or wait until another professor taught the course before signing up.

Getting Assistance from Parents

Often beginning as early as elementary school, parents provided considerable academic assistance to their children with learning disabilities. Whether formally labeled or not, students reported that parents became very involved with their education, providing tutors, reviewing homework, editing and typing papers, and selecting teachers and classes. Such assistance was prevalent, not limited to a few parents.

Students reported receiving the most parental help with their writing assignments, especially during elementary and high school. Some people also mentioned having to bring home weekly performance reports from each of their classes for their parents' scrutiny. Most students prefaced their remarks by noting that their parents didn't do their work for them. In many cases, however, parental assistance appeared to go beyond what might be considered typical assistance levels. Many people stated that they had depended on their parents "heavily," some reporting their parents "practically writing their papers." One student described the extent of his parents' involvement with his schoolwork:

My dad helped me with all of my math, algebra, and geometry, and my mom helped with spelling and writing. I started bringing things home before high school. In high school my mother went over every paper I wrote. They'd have a weekly report sent home from my counselor telling them if I was falling behind, and pointing out where I needed help. All these reports would be pinned to the refrigerator, reminding me to bring home the books I was having trouble with. My parents really did get me through high school. I even remember bringing home papers during college.

Another student recalled that she had "always needed my parents to help me write papers." Noting that her father would never actually do the work for her, she indicated that his help was "life-saving":

With reports and stuff, I always needed somebody. When I wrote a paper, my father would dictate the words to me. I'd sit there for hours while he read a chapter, explained the whole thing to me, and then we'd answer questions about it. He also made me go to a tutor twice a week every summer. He was very strict about that. He's still making sure I have tutors in college.

Another student told a similar story about her parents, especially her father, who had provided significant help for her during high school:

I don't know what I would have done if I'd had another father. My poor father never had any idea he'd end up as my proofreader. He proofread everything, and if something had to be typed, my mother typed it. If I wrote a paper my father didn't like, he would rewrite it a little bit for me, switch things around, and make it sound better. In my first few years of high school I always got checked, and my papers rewritten. Once in social studies class we had to read some newspaper articles, so my dad picked out some articles for me. We discussed them and I brought them to school. Another time I had to write a paper on the anatomy of the knee and I didn't have a clue as to what these gigantic words meant. I went to my dad and he took me to the library. We found some books and he helped me write the paper.

Not all parental assistance was limited to tutorial and remedial intervention. In several cases students recalled that their parents had intervened with counselors, principals, and teachers about schedules, courses, and assignments. In one situation a young woman described how her mother's involvement went beyond supplemental instruction:

My mother is a manipulative woman. She deliberately became head of the PTO throughout my education so that she could handpick my teachers. She deliberately stayed in power until I was finished with each level, all the way through high school. My brother, who was two years ahead of me, used to give her all the inside reports on the best teachers.

For the most part, parents reduced their direct assistance when their children went to college. Some, however, extended their participation, maintaining weekly contacts and/or regularly discussing accommodations with the college's academic support personnel. Several students, especially those who commuted to college, persuaded parents to continue editing and typing their college papers. One student, returning home for vacation, persuaded his mother to help him research and write a term paper:

My mother went to Philadelphia and got the information I needed from the library. Then she and I sat down and wrote three drafts of the paper. We started Friday night and finished up Sunday. I got a B+. I did better than some friends who were A students and had been researching their papers for months.

Many people mentioned that they also received emotional support from their families. Some referred to their parent's participation as "handholding," or, as in the following situation, "cheerleading":

My dad used to get me all pumped up. He'd try to get me psyched up to go to school. He used to tell me I had a mission to go to school and to learn. Even now when I feel down about something, or I'm doing bad in class, he says, "Don't worry about it. Try your hardest. Do your best." Anytime I feel kind of low, I call him. He still tells me I'm doing great things, that I'm doing well, and that I'm going to succeed.

Another person described periods of discouragement when he would come home and tell his parents that he could not do college work. During these times, he remembered, his parents were "almost like coaches, pushing me to keep going." He noted that his parents weren't "good students themselves, but they could understand my problems, and could deal with my mind."

Getting Assistance from Siblings and Spouses

Parents were not the only source of family assistance. Several individuals reported that brothers and sisters also could be especially helpful. One person recalled her older brother inviting her to study with him when her parents were "on her case about grades." Numerous other people described older siblings who would give them the benefit of their upper class experiences and help them study for tests.

Spouses were mentioned as important sources of help for individuals in college. In most cases spouses provided the same kind of assistance persons received from parents, siblings, and friends, such as in studying, exam preparation, proofreading, typing, and writing. In one instance a man's wife helped him with his spelling and reading:

> My wife can spell, and that's where I use her. She can't cook, but that's life. I'll ask her to read something, and I throw her a lot of stuff to read to me because I literally don't have time to sit down and do everything they send me in the mail and in my classes.

Another individual recalled his wife's critical help in preparing for exams:

> Without my wife I would never have been able to make it through this course. In the medical technology course we were tested every class. My wife and I would get a pile of about 20 old exams and sit there for hours and read questions to each other.

Getting Assistance from Peers

Although peers could be socially rejecting in elementary and high schools, they could also be valuable accomplices. One young woman recounted that in elementary school "the girls I was with knew that I hated to read aloud so they helped me out by volunteering to read for me." The student also recalled that while her friends continued to accept and help her, they were baffled by her behavior as they got older. She stated: "When I reached high school, the kids didn't really understand why I would be missing words. Like when I would write a note, there would be words missing and it wouldn't be clear. And they would wonder why."

One person explained that he did not want to tell anyone about his learning disabilities and always "felt bad about having to scheme ways of getting around things." In high school he relied on a close friend who "was really good at every subject. I sort of latched onto him and talked to him a lot about my writing or math assignments."

Although one young woman "felt bad about always depending on her friends for help," she reported how she sometimes appealed to her friends' sympathies. "Sometimes I would come across as such a poor student and just look so pathetic that my friends would say, 'Oh, don't worry about it. Here, let me do it for you.'"

One student used her friends covertly to overcome her poor reading skills by asking them about assigned books and then listening to their discussion:

> You don't have to read books in high school if you don't want to. I hung around with a lot of students who thought a lot. They were all well read, and they'd check out books and talk about them. They just naturally did that. It never occurred to me to do that, but I would check out a book, fight my way through it and then I'd listen to them talk about it. So I really learned a lot from my peers in junior high and high school.

About two thirds of the college students in the study relied on the assistance of fellow students to succeed academically. This contrasted with the kind of help secured by high school students, who relied more heavily on their families.

In many cases students with learning disabilities sought out those whom they judged to be the brightest students in their classes and attempted to get their help in securing class notes, editing and typing papers, and reviewing for tests. As one Jewish student wryly joked: "The critical question when you met a girl you liked used to be, 'Are you Jewish?' Now it's, 'Can you type?'" One person who did not want to accept formal accommodations described how she had gotten her boyfriend and roommates to help her:

> I couldn't accept accommodations because it would have singled me out as different. My second year of college, I ran into trouble because I had to write term papers. My boyfriend would see me struggling and he'd say, "Let me help you." He wrote my term papers for me and protected me in that way. He thought it was funny but I just had no idea of how to begin. In high school I just copied my papers from books or was part of a group project. My roommates would see me get the typewriter out and say, "Let me do it for you." So they would type the papers.

Sometimes assistance did not come so easily. Students with learning disabilities believed that they had to demonstrate their worthiness to other students in order to elicit their help. This often meant that they could not miss classes—which they rarely did anyway—and that they carefully prepared for class, took detailed notes, and/or participated actively in class. One student, thus, demonstrated his competence to his classmates in order to obtain their assistance:

> I'm a good judge of people, and can tell who the real smart ones are by seeing that this kid has been sitting in the front row or this one hasn't been doing anything all semester. I'll go up to the person and say that I'm not a good note-taker and was wondering if I could use your notes. Most of the time people have been more than happy to help, because I've really worked myself up to being one of the most respected students in class. I'm a big class participant because I try to make up for my tests, so they can say this kid knows his stuff even though he doesn't take tests well. So I sit in the first or second row, right in front of the teacher. Sometimes I've even taught a class for the teacher, so people know I'm not flaking off. It's a strategy for how to work with people. It's like patting someone on the back and saying, "Hey, look, why don't we get together and talk it [the course material] out. Maybe we can put together some of these things and really do well on the test." Usually they are as excited about it [studying together] as I am.

Another student used his note-taking ability to secure the cooperation of other students for a group study:

> My strategy is notes. It's everything to me. People are amazed at my notes. I have a bad memory, so I make a point of going through the notes from beginning to end with one or two people. That's important for them, because I'm usually the one that has all the notes, because I never miss class and I make sure I have everything. But going over the notes verbally really helps me remember them, so it's the studying with others that's important to me, too. I really depend on studying in groups.

Minimizing and Avoiding Family Involvement

While many people could not manage their academic work without their family's remedial and/or emotional support, others resented or rejected such assistance and wanted to manage their difficulties themselves. In some situations people did not agree with their parents' methods of help. One young woman had rebelled against her father's tendency to take over her work: "If I wrote a paper my father didn't like, he'd try to rewrite it and use words I didn't know [the meaning of]. If the teacher asked me what these words meant, I wouldn't know. So I took them out."

Another individual resented the pressure his parents put on him to study harder, when he felt that he was doing as much as he could:

> My parents were always pushing me to do better. To this day my father always says, "You can do better." But can I do better? I can only study so much. My mother keeps saying, "Practice makes perfect. Practice makes perfect." But for me practice doesn't make perfect. Practice makes worse.

One young man described how his mother "went overboard" in his behalf:

> I was having trouble in biology, and my mother began calling up my teacher, who I didn't get along with anyway. They started having fights on the phone. I hated that. I hated it when she called up any of my teachers. I felt paranoid and embarrassed. So finally I told her not to call my teacher anymore.

In some cases people reported being sick of hearing about, thinking about, and doing schoolwork. As one individual said: "My mother tried to take me aside after school, but school was over. I had heard enough and done enough. I was free. Don't bother me with any more tutoring."

Whether they accepted or rejected family help, most people reported many arguments about grades and studying. Moreover, most individuals resented and resisted parental interventions at some level. Some openly expressed hostility toward parents, whereas others internalized their anger. One student recalled that "there were many screaming matches in my family over school." Reflecting a more internalized response, another student related:

> I would write a first draft and bring it home to mommy. She would correct it, and little Jimmy would rewrite it. As Jimmy was rewriting it, mommy would be telling him how to spell certain words. It was very irritating, but the grades were better when mommy helped me.

People's reactions to such assistance also reflected anxiety and confusion regarding what their academic difficulties and familial dependence meant for their personal identity, future autonomy, and intellectual competence—all particularly sensitive issues for young adults. Despite their resistance and anxiety, however, most had privately admitted that they needed such help, eventually resigned themselves to it, and indicated, sometimes reluctantly, that it had probably helped them. One student remarked, "I would never hand in any written work that my parents didn't check," and another noted that "my parents seemed like the only people who knew what was wrong or could help me."

The bulk of family assistance apparently tapered off when students entered college. The vast majority of college students in the study reportedly relied on the assistance of fellow students and/or the college's support services, and rarely mentioned their family as a primary source of help.

ABSENCE OR WITHDRAWAL OF FAMILY ASSISTANCE

A few people stated that they had received little or no support from their families. In some cases parents were unsupportive both before and after their son or daughter was labeled. One young woman commented:

> My parents were just not supportive. Whatever they did seemed to be wrong. They didn't know how to help me and mostly ended up badgering me. I went through these terrible emotional sessions where they would holler at me: "How come you don't know this word? We've told it to you six times."

After she was diagnosed, reportedly her parents' attitude changed very little. She pointed out: "My father knew that I needed professional help, but he was angry about it; angry with me for being different, for being less than perfect."

Such comments were rare but not altogether isolated. Several persons reported that they came from high-achieving families where poor academic performance was rare and rarely understood. One student described her parents as "geniuses who couldn't understand how their kid could have a problem." In another situation, a young woman described her father's attitude as sympathetic but patronizing:

> My father accepted the situation. That's the best way to describe it. He never understood me. He would say, "Poor kid, she tries hard, but it's that damn learning disability." Someone would ask him

what it was and he wouldn't know, but he'd say that "we try to give her everything she needs so she won't suffer too much."

Several individuals described disparate family reactions to their difficulties. One young woman noted that although her mother's advocacy efforts on her behalf were extremely helpful, the rest of her family didn't understand her difficulties. Several people recalled their siblings as outstanding students who had ignored them and thought they were lazy. In one situation, a person described his older brother and sister as particularly hostile toward him. Apparently, they had been placed in the embarrassing predicament of being called to his classroom, where his elementary school teacher had pointed out his sloppy work and messy desk.

When persons discussed the differences between high school and college, they frequently mentioned the withdrawal of parental support that had occurred when they left for college. It is not known whether parents of non-learning-disabled students are equally involved in their children's education, or whether this level of assistance is helpful or harmful. Apparently, however, many people with learning disabilities initially believed that they could not succeed in college without family help. As one individual noted: "I thought my parents would always be there." Another student, who "would have probably dropped out of high school if I had had another father," also elected a college close to her father, "who seemed to be the only person who really understood me."

SUMMARY

A major task confronting high school and college students with learning disabilities was managing their academic requirements. Most schools and colleges had formal, well-defined procedures for providing those students academic assistance. Some institutions even had techniques for managing those "suspected" of being learning disabled. Succeeding in educational institutions, however, encompassed more than achieving academic success and required more than obtaining formal academic accommodations and following prescribed remedial dictates. In fact, formal institutional procedures sometimes exacerbated people's problems and interfered with their desires and ability to manage their problems on their own terms.

In their quest to succeed academically, students also had to understand and manage the social and psychological dilemmas that accompanied the formal programs of remediation. Specifically, they had to learn how to control and manage information about themselves, through selective concealing and revealing, in order to minimize the stigma associated with special help. Information management was often easier to accomplish in college, where students enjoyed more personal and programmatic autonomy than they were allowed in elementary and high school. However, formal accommodations such as untimed tests, time extensions, and tutoring required a degree of public identification as learning disabled that many individuals were unwilling to accept. Using such services also necessitated gaining the cooperation of course instructors who were sometimes skeptical of, and resistant to, special provisions. This is not to say that formal accommodations were not helpful. In many cases they were extremely helpful. In numerous cases, however, they were viewed as insufficiently helpful to warrant public disclosure of disability. Consequently, students modified, avoided or minimized formal accommodations; circumvented the procedures offered to them through their college's special services office; rejected affiliations with special staff, departments, and organizations; and devised covert strategies for securing help on their own terms. Some people accepted formal accommodations only if they could do so on a course-by-course basis and could ensure instructor cooperation and their own privacy.

Considerable professional and investigative attention has been directed toward accurate clinical diagnosis, and toward the provision of formal accommodative and remedial services to persons with learning disabilities. Often neglected are the stigma, the social and psychological dilemmas, and the consequent individual adjustments that accompany formal, remedial, and accommodative procedures. It is likely that officially sanctioned activities represent only a small part of how people labeled as learning disabled respond to the people, tasks, and settings around them, and ultimately exert control over their own lives. Such control must also include management over the ways they are defined and treated, and the social roles they are expected to play by those around them.

4

Getting Along Socially

Being learning disabled has been termed a social disability (Brown, 1985; Gresham, 1988; Lerner, 1985), often resulting in unsatisfactory child and adult peer relationships (see also Hallahan et al., 1985, pp. 147–148). Citing recent research, Lerner (1985) noted that "learning disabled children do not do well in dealing with people" (p. 468). She stated that learning disabled youngsters make more competitive statements, receive more rejections, are less cooperative, and are more deferential and hostile than their nondisabled peers. Lerner also concluded that learning disabled students often behave in socially inappropriate ways, and are "at risk for social neglect and rejection" (p. 468).

Gresham (1988) reviewed the literature on social competence and motivational characteristics of children with learning disabilities and concluded that they are "poorly accepted, neglected, or rejected by their nonhandicapped peers" (p. 296). He recommended that, as such findings suggest, students with learning disabilities "are in need of specially designed instructional programs to remediate social skill deficits to facilitate peer acceptance" (p. 296). After reviewing the literature on teacher and peer attitudes toward children with learning disabilities, Reid (1984, p. 168) concluded that (a) regular teachers attached a negative stereotype to the label "learning disability"; (b) children with learning disabilities have significantly lower social standing than nondisabled peers; and (c) regular teachers and nondisabled peers behave more negatively toward learning disabled children than they do toward typical students. Although Reid qualified these findings because of methodological flaws and inadequately explored questions in the available research, she concurred that children with learning disabilities are often placed in settings that are socially hostile and unsupportive, leading her to question whether mainstreaming was doing more social and psychological harm than good.

The literature on adolescents and adults seems more equivocal than that on children. Kavale (1988), for example, reviewed the literature and found follow-up studies on social/behavioral functioning were about evenly split between positive and negative outcomes. Brown (1985) contended that "many learning disabled adults have trouble meeting people, working with others, and making friends. They do not fit in easily" (p. 32). She concluded that social skill deficiencies are an integral part of the learning disabilities problem. Perlmutter, Crocker, Cordray, and Garstecki (1983) have found that learning disabled adolescents were less accepted overall than non-disabled students. They also observed that most students with learning disabilities were rated neutrally by their peers, and some were well liked. Sabornie (1983) reported that learning disabled students attending regular high school classes were as well accepted as their non-disabled peers. Moreover, Falfard and Haubrick (1981) followed up high school graduates and found that most were involved in a variety of social relationships. Warner, Alley, and Deschler (1980), and Deschler and Schumaker (1983), although concluding that adolescents with learning disabilities were not socially isolated, indicated that they participated in fewer extracurricular activities and socialized less with friends than their non-learning-disabled peers.

This chapter explores how persons labeled as learning disabled viewed their social relationships. Particular attention is paid to peer relationships, and to how individuals described and managed these relationships in various settings.

IN ELEMENTARY AND HIGH SCHOOL

Experiencing Social Stigma

Bad grades. Whether or not they had been labeled as learning disabled, people recalled that their peer relations sometimes suffered because of their inability to "measure up." Several individuals remembered being teased in elementary school. A young woman remembered having been teased and, in response, attempting to explain her problem without much success. In response to classmate tauntings— "Naah, naah, naah, you can't read anything but baby books"—and to questions about why she couldn't read, she had replied that something was wrong in her genes. Despite her explanation, however, she was still teased.

One individual believed that his early academic experiences had adversely affected both his peer relations and his later social and psychological development:

I repeated first grade and lost a lot of friends because of that. It didn't affect me so much then. It's only later on that I think it influenced the way I am. I'm not a group-oriented person. I'm an individual person, and I don't like hanging out in groups. I'm not a very trusting person. I don't trust people totally. You have to show me that I can trust you.

Along with many recollections of elementary school social experiences, students also described incidents that occurred as they got older, and their attempts to control and manage social embarrassment. One young man, to avoid reading aloud in class, began to come to class late, or to seat himself away from those persons who were supposed to read. One person informed his ninth-grade teacher that he was no longer going to read aloud in class. Another individual began to withdraw from her old friends and find new ones, because "their intuitive summation of me was that I was less than they were. They thought I was thicker than thick."

Special placements. As often as they linked negative peer reactions to poor academic performance, individuals associated their social devaluation with special classes. For many, such placements only exaggerated their problems and caused the most stigmatizing reactions from peers.

Although poor grades made people feel different and often incompetent, many labeled and nonlabeled students got bad grades and still succeeded socially. However, school actions such as placement in special programs for the handicapped not only separated students from their friends and made them feel different, but at a most self-conscious time of life, publicly certified them as globally inferior. Such assigned status was not lost on peers, who reportedly reacted in various ways. As one young woman remembered: "The kids at school used to really chastise me. They called me brain damaged because I went to this skills lab." Another individual noted that remedial class placement operationally defined for him the difference between being a poor student and being stupid:

In earlier grades I was getting upset with the fact that they sent me to other places. I went to the learning center and the principal's office. I wasn't doing as well as anyone else, especially my two sisters. But in high school I started taking all the remedial classes, and this was the point at which I thought I was stupid. I was in with these kids that were slow. It was obvious it was a slow class, and I wasn't in any of the classes with my friends.

Special class placements provided students with numerous messages of inferiority, one of which was separation from their friends. One person described the phenomenon this way:

It was kind of like a message. It was a smaller room. You weren't with your friends. At first I didn't know that most of the kids had learning disabilities. I thought they put me in a smaller class because the other [class] was too big. I was told to go to this one room and there was a lady in charge of the resource room, and she was telling them what their problem was. I was 13 at the time, and for a kid who's 13, that's a lot of peer pressure. It was like changing and starting all over again. And [thinking people were saying] "He goes to that room. He's dumb, stupid." It kind of got to me.

Numerous students emphasized that placement in special classes was more socially stigmatizing and psychologically demoralizing than getting bad grades. As noted in chapter 2, several people tried to camouflage their problems by acting out so as to be seen as "tough" by peers, rather than be called stupid. One individual recalled:

I had problems in school ever since I was set back in first grade. They used to pull me out of class away from other students, and I'd go into a room with just me and another teacher. Then I'd go back into the regular class and end up failing. The other students would know what was going on. Rather than be called stupid, I would cause trouble. Rather than have the other kids call me stupid, I'd put on the tough act. A lot of kids called me names because they moved along and I stayed back. But I could put on the tough act because I had the age and size on them. And it got to the point where they finally said, "Let's leave the guy alone." The tough act was the only way to stop being called an idiot or being picked on.

Several persons noted a preference for staying back rather than being placed in special classes. One individual explained:

They had this tutor thing where you'd go to LD classes. It was kind of hard being in those classes because you were looked at like a stupid person or something. I went to those so-called LD classes for one year, and the next year I took regular classes mixed in with LD classes. I took no learning disability classes my last year, but I had to stay back a year.

A young woman recalled the stigma of being assigned to a specialist who also worked with students labeled as mentally retarded. She remembered this as worse than being held out of class or staying back:

I spent a lot of time out of the classroom. I was sent to the nurse's office and principal's office to do my work. I was held back, and my mother made sure I got an LD specialist, and I hated it. I dreaded walking down that long hall to that specialist because retarded children went there.

Special class placements also revealed differences that had been unnoticed or unimportant outside of school.

It was hard to go to the resource room. It's a social thing, I guess. I was separate from most of the other people in school, and that hits you more in high school, because those are the impression years. People asked me why I went [to the resource room], and when I told them I had a learning disability they didn't believe me. They said, "How could you?" The big question was, "How come you get to take your tests in another room and have a long time?" I guess they expected someone with a learning disability to be like a handicapped person, but there's nothing visibly wrong with me so it was hard for them to believe it.

Another individual noted the difference between her "in-school" and her "out-of-school" social experiences and self-perceptions:

It was very hard seeing my friends go past me in school. They were taking advanced classes, and I was with the "bad" people in the slower classes. In school I was with all these people, yet after school I felt normal again. I was back with all my friends and everything was nice again. Sometimes it would bother me. I would get angry at myself and wonder why I couldn't be doing the same things as my friends; why couldn't I be in the same classes. That upset me, and I used to get extremely down on myself.

Some students reported not only going from the regular class to special placements, but sometimes returning from special to regular classes. This kind of turmoil and ambiguity was reportedly difficult to

deal with, socially and psychologically, especially when a return to the
regular class was not accompanied by academic improvement. One
individual recounted very intense feelings about such an experience:

> In the fourth grade the teacher noticed that I had been passed
> along. She suggested that I go to this learning disabilities place, a
> special training place in a separate building. In seventh grade I was
> still far behind everyone, but they put me back in the regular class
> because they didn't know what else to do. In science class they gave
> me a different book because I couldn't read the regular book. I did
> a bit better, but still was barely passing.
>
> I was kind of ashamed because I wasn't doing things the way
> everybody else was. After the special class, then back to the regular
> class, then all the trouble in science [class]. It was at that point that I
> realized I was a hell of a lot different than the others. Being 12 or 13,
> it really started to hit home. I remember a really intense depression
> and suicidal thoughts at that age. I didn't understand what this thing
> was. I was feeling horrible, hanging around the bright kids, but
> having to go to the not-so-bright classes.

Symbols of inferiority. Special class placement was not the only
stimulus for social devaluation and psychological demoralization. Located in regular classrooms were various symbols of inferiority such as
special reading books, different test levels, and various accommodations. All of these provided social signals to others and were remembered clearly by many students. One student recalled having "these
specially colored reading books, and someone would say, 'Are you still
in the yellow book?' I would tell them that I was still in the yellow
book, and they'd say, 'Are you stupid?' It made me angry as hell."

A young woman recalled the social stigma of taking a different
level of tests in class:

> I remember in the sixth grade taking the sras. I was always in the
> front row, in the lower group. I didn't like that test at all. Everyone
> would go up and get their sras and they'd be getting blue colored
> ones and I'd be getting red. So there were things that really sepa-
> rated you out; little activities in school and functions that you could
> see there was a difference between what the other kids were doing
> and what you were doing.

In several circumstances individuals in regular classrooms were
confronted with stigmatizing accommodations. One student remem-

bered being teased by others, both because he couldn't read aloud very well and because he had been assigned a tutor to help correct the problem. He had the tutor "until around eighth grade, and I did not want the tutor anymore. I didn't want the other kids hassling me." Another individual mentioned being self-conscious about a tape recorder that he used to help him record class notes, but which precipitated "a lot of smart remarks, and made me feel out of place."

Escaping Social Stigma

Numerous individuals recalled no particular social stigma associated with their learning disabilities during elementary or secondary school. Some people characterized themselves as loners and felt more comfortable doing things by themselves. Others felt that although their friends were aware of their academic problems, they still remained friends. A few stated that going to the resource room required some getting used to, but they believed that any negative consequences of special placements and services were worth it because of the help they received. One individual with reading difficulties remarked that he did not remember being picked on or discriminated against in high school. He did not think his friends looked at him any differently, but that "I just knew that my learning situation was different. Whereas they could sit down and read a book, and know all the facts, I'd have to start maybe a week or two ahead and keep reading, and sometimes reread."

Another student, who was not formally diagnosed until college but who had received poor grades and been placed in "slow" classes, indicated that her school problems had affected her social standing minimally. She reported that her friends were "just nice, normal, and bright and would never say anything negative. They'd say, 'Whatever is better for you.' They were great people and still are. My group of friends never changed. I was always accepted by them and went to their parties."

Several individuals reported that their friends had brushed off their disability by pointing out their positive attributes and declaring that everyone has strengths and weaknesses. One young woman recalled that her friends had excused her disability because they believed she was lazy or "was making these problems up" in order to get out of work. Although her friends recognized that she was a little behind academically, they pointed to her good looks and the fact that she had a boyfriend as indices of her worth. Another person mentioned that his friends paid more attention to his social than his academic skills. He

wonder about my significance of age of being diagnosed

remarked that he had always had very close friends: "I've tended to be a strong person, keeping my friends up. When you're keeping people up, it's only natural for them to help you stay afloat."

Some students felt that their disability and special placement had minimal, negative social effects when handled properly. For one person this meant waiting for the right moment, telling only trusted friends, and enrolling in a program that included valued students:

> It [the resource room] helps in the long run. It's also just growing up. I really didn't tell my close friends until I thought they were mature. I waited until like junior year when they found out that not everyone in there had a learning disability. Some athletes used it, and some folks came in because there were computers in the room. People used it who were having trouble with a certain subject, or someone needed to type something.

A few students who believed that special placements did draw negative attention from their peers asserted that the help they received from their special programming was nonetheless too valuable to give up. One person thought his friends were jealous of the assistance he received from the resource room. Reportedly, they had wondered why they too couldn't use the room, since they often experienced academic problems and might also have a learning disability.

Some people pointed to some lucky circumstances that had enabled them to escape social stigma by eluding detection. One student, for example, explained that she was young for her grade and had moved around a lot during her school years, both of which served as a rationale for her mediocre grades. A young man believed that his learning disability had gone undiscovered because he had attended a poor school with unmotivated students. By comparison, his grades had seemed good. A young woman felt that she had experienced minimal stigma because she went to a large school. Another student reported that she had avoided detection only because her school had emphasized group projects: "I knew that I wasn't up to the level of my peers, but we did things in groups. We did group projects, and so that's how I got through public school."

Managing Social Stigma

Students employed several tactics for dealing with the social consequences surrounding their academic problems. Some individuals camouflaged their problems, some attempted to emphasize and excel in certain activities, and some solicited and received help from friends to overcome their difficulties.

Faking it. Many students tried to get by without telling their friends about their problems, or by minimizing the extent of their difficulties. People employed a variety of strategies for avoiding behaviors, labels, placements, or other signs of what they considered social inferiority. Several persons tried to cover their bad grades or special placement with deceit and/or evasion. One individual had blamed her problems on her parents for placing her in special classes during high school. Another had claimed to be avoiding certain classes because she didn't like them:

> Friends would ask why I wasn't taking a foreign language. I used to say, "Oh, I just don't want to." If I had said I was learning disabled, it just wouldn't have worked. I didn't tell any friends. None of my friends knew I had it [LD] until the end of college.

Several students would brush off their poor performance, giving others the impression that they could do their work if they really wanted to, but preferred to be lazy or funny. One individual recalled "faking through" an oral reading task in elementary school by making up a story rather than reading it:

> I was supposed to be reading these books about frogs aloud in class. But I couldn't read. So when it came my turn I just made up a story from the pictures. All the kids thought it was great. So it was like a defense, because I knew I couldn't do it so I just did something else.

One student attempted to define his problem in a way that avoided both the stigma of difference and any suspicion that he was seeking favored treatment:

> If anyone asked me, I usually just said I have problems reading and writing. People don't really need to know, and you don't want them to know it. You'd just like to be in the same situation as the other students. I'm not going to go out of my way to tell them because some of them say, "Well, what are you going to do, make up for bad grades?"

Another person tried to give his friends the impression that he was doing all right, and that he wasn't particularly worried about his problems. As other people also noted, friends often were aware of the difficulties:

> Because most people didn't see me in class, I would never tell anybody. If someone was talking about how easy a test was I'd just say, "no problem," even though I got a D. My friends understood. I don't know what they really thought. Now they say that they didn't think I was stupid. I was in a few classes with them and I would hate it because it was so embarrassing. When I was found out [being in the same classes] I made a joke about it. I'd say, "I'm backwards," but they'd help me and they knew I was having problems.

One student initially blamed his special placement on his parents. Although he eventually concluded that his peers knew that he attended special classes, he had avoided telling all but his closest friends about his diagnosed disability because "I didn't want them to know and think that I was different. My friends never asked, but I knew they knew why I was going to resource. I never told anyone I had LD except two friends who also had it. None of us went around telling people we had this problem."

Although most strategies were designed to camouflage school-related problems, several people recalled having to cover up persistent extraschool predicaments. One young man had patronized fast-food restaurants so that he wouldn't have to read the menu in front of his friends. When he went to unfamiliar restaurants, he would pretend to read the menu but would order what his friends ordered, or something he remembered from another restaurant. His social strategy was to stay alert, noting that "you can learn so much from listening and hearing, and you can compensate for everything. You can become so acute and so sharp about what is going on in your surroundings. You take in everything you can't read."

Another student also remembered devising special cues for herself to avoid potentially embarrassing social situations. To differentiate her left hand from her right, she wore two rings on one hand. During her driver education classes she had "almost killed the driver ed teacher and everyone else in the car because [she] didn't know left from right." Her cues also helped her during soccer games when her coach would tell her "to go play left fullback." Of course, when all else failed, she recommended "playing a little stupid and no one would pick up on your learning disability."

With a little help from my family. As noted in earlier chapters of this book, families of persons with learning disabilities often provided key academic, vocational, and emotional support. In most instances such support was directed toward assisting an individual to succeed in school or at work. In some cases, however, family assistance was intended to bolster a person's social standing. In one example, an older brother had allowed his younger brother to associate with him and his friends to heighten his younger brother's social status. In another circumstance a person who had spent a lot of time in special classes and tutorial sessions related that her mother had started a Girl Scout troop:

> She began the troop so that I could get to know the other kids in my grade. She became the scout leader and got all the girls in my grade to join. It was the best troop, and that's how I got to know my classmates. By fifth grade I knew everyone, and that was a good social thing, too. They remembered me from the Girl Scout troop, and got me involved with all of the girls. When I got to junior high school, I knew everyone.

Finding a strong suit. Many individuals pointed to activities they did well as ways of managing the negative consequences of their academic deficiencies. One person recalled that his automotive repair skills served to boost his self-esteem and social standing:

> Once I made some friends around school, I'd walk into their house and see that they were doing calculus, and that would really put me down, make me feel bad. But sometimes it evened out. Like one friend was having trouble with his car and he only knew how to check the oil and the transmission fluid, and that was it. So I went all through the car explaining to him how to do certain things. He didn't know much about cars and I didn't know much about calculus, so there was never any trouble between us.

Another student mentioned several extracurricular functions as important, compensatory activities:

One of the ways I helped improve my self-image was success outside of the classroom. I got involved in the television club, and in high school I produced my own TV shows. I broadcasted the football games, did camera work, and acted on these shows. The shows were broadcast on cable TV, so you could see something done that I had a hand in. I knew that I was successful at what I did, and that really helped change my attitude. I also joined the Dungeons and Dragons club. I was one of the best players, and people always wanted to play with me because I had good ideas. If you have success in your extracurricular activities, it takes your mind off school, and you get positive feedback.

Several people pointed to their sports achievements as ways to "show off" and thereby enhance their social standing and sense of personal accomplishment. One young man recalled: "The only friends I had in school were on the baseball team. I mean I had to be good at something. I couldn't do school." Extracurricular proficiencies often made people feel better about themselves, but they did not always guarantee social acceptance. As one individual noted: "In elementary school I excelled in sports and got most of my satisfaction from sports and lunch. But I don't remember being terribly popular." Another student recalled a similar experience: "Everyone looked up to me when I was on the baseball field, but no one talked to me much any other time." A third person saw her artistic skill as an important competency, but a limited source of attention and acceptance from peers. In art class she remembered constructing "these massive bodies while other kids were trying to do these stupid things I could laugh at. I had so many pieces displayed in elementary school, and everyone would ask me, 'How do you do that?' So I compensated there, but that was only one hour out of the day."

Students consistently expressed a desire to show their competency to their friends in some areas of school life. Although proficiency in any or all socially valued areas did not guarantee high peer acceptance, the absence of demonstrable competencies in these areas could prove particularly isolating. As one individual pointed out:

In high school I felt very alone. I felt shoved away in a corner, and I have some bitter feelings about high school. If you weren't good at sports or academics, they did very little to help you. I took a lot of peer pressure. If I spelled something wrong, they'd laugh and kid me about it; regular kid's stuff. I couldn't turn around and say, "Yeah, but I can do this."

IN COLLEGE

Maintaining Privacy

I've told a few close friends. Although college students were often part of a large student body, they still felt that privacy was difficult to maintain. Regardless of when they were diagnosed and how severe their high school academic problems had been, most of the college students said that they attempted to control information about their learning disability or poor academic performance. As one person said: "I don't go around telling people I have a learning disability, like I had a cold or something." Another individual stated: "It's something I have to deal with, not them, so I keep it mostly inside. I've told maybe one or two people up here [at college] who are really close friends. They were nice about it. No one asked me to go into details or anything."

Several people who described themselves as cautious about whom they told remembered having been hurt by others' reactions. One person who told only very close friends about his problem remarked that he was "very protective of myself. If I do tell somebody, they have gotten inside the cement wall I build around myself. It's a hard cocoon."

A young man described some reasons for his social caution:

> I've been screwed over by a lot of kids. Now I'm a very good judge of character, and I don't tell people [about my LD] who I don't think can handle it. I never told anyone [about my LD] until my senior year of high school. Then I told two or three people. Last year I told three people—my roommate and two girls who I am friendly with. This year I'm telling more people. I don't know how I decide who to tell. It's like a gut feeling, I guess. If I think this person is interested in me as a person and really wants to know, I'll tell him. I make a mistake every so often. Like I told a guy, and he says to his friends to stay away from me because I'm dyslexic. It's easier to tell a guy. I'm dating a girl now, and I haven't told her because I don't feel that she would understand. She'd pretend to understand. If I continue to see her, I'm going to have to tell her.

The preceding comments reflect a prevalent trait among college students to wait until they had developed a friendship before telling another person about their learning disabilities. Thus, some categorized their associates according to those they told and those they didn't tell. One student told only her best friends, not including her sorority sisters:

> I don't tell everyone. I don't tell people in my sorority. I never thought about it. I wouldn't know who to tell. I'm sure everyone suffers the social aspects. A big thing in society is to be accepted, and I'm sure that people think that [other] people will look down on them and won't be their friend. That crosses everyone's mind; but I choose to tell my friends, and I figure if they can't accept that, they aren't really my friends. I accept their faults, why shouldn't they accept my differences? Often my friends don't believe me when I tell them, but they say okay, if you say so.

Some people measured their learning disability in terms of its consequences. If the social consequences could be controlled, the disability was seen as no longer existing. One person described this view:

> In class I participate a lot. So even if I don't get great grades, I'm perceived that way. In class I always get Bs and never As. One time I got a B and surprised someone who thought I was going to get an A. I thought, "Good. I fooled her."
>
> As far as the learning disability, I never think of it as a problem socially. I'm probably one of the better socializers. If I see a girl I like, I'll approach her and hang out for a while just talking. My roommates and I have been together for 4 years. All good students, and we look at each other as equals. To them it's kind of like, so what. One of my roommates, who can read a book and remember it the next day, doesn't look at me and say "Oh, you can't do that." It's like, "This is how you read, let me show you how I read." He helps me out on those things. We kid around. I'd say, "Oh, I have learning disability; I can't do this." They see mail sent to all LD students, which I don't open. If you went up to any of them and asked if they knew anyone with learning disability they'd immediately say no. They wouldn't even think about saying yes when it comes to me. Eventually they might say, "Oh yeah, my roommate is one." It's just not a problem in their heads. So I don't consider I have it anymore.

They think I'm faking. As noted in earlier chapters, accommodations and special arrangements provided to alleviate student's academic problems could themselves cause social stigma. Some individuals believed that receiving accommodations could not only advertise their disability, but lead to questions about their honesty. One person worried that people who "don't see anything wrong with me, then see me getting extra help, may think, 'Oh, give me a break. You could do the work without this extra time.'" A young woman reported having experienced the suspicion and resentment of even her closest friends:

> I told some of my closest friends. And a lot of people doubted me after I started getting my grades back and I was doing better than everyone else. They said, "Like, right, you're really disabled!" And I didn't like that kind of comment because it made me feel like I was really cheating the system. Some of my classmates think I've made up this whole story; they just don't understand.

Having a learning disability could also lead to certain institutional privileges that some students preferred to keep hidden from their friends. One person explained that because of her disability, she was granted placement priority in classes that were in great demand and therefore were closed to many nonmajors or other students. Because this benefit could cause some resentment among their friends, students who took advantage of the privilege often claimed that they "talked their way into the class."

I don't care who knows. Several persons stated that they did not care who knew about their learning disability, noting that they frequently mentioned it during normal social discourse:

> I've never hidden it [LD]. To me, it's just the way I am. If you like it, great. If you don't, then find somebody else. I guess there are people who look down on people in my position. It's not such a big deal when I tell somebody. It's just part of the conversation where one thing leads to another. Like telling someone I'm having trouble in class, I might say it's probably because of my learning disability. That's how it would come out.

Other people noted that it made little difference to them what others thought of them, except for their friends. And as one person indicated, many of his friends shared similar problems: "I was never one to worry about what other people thought. Most of my friends are computer folks, and they can't spell or write either." Another individual publicly declared herself as learning disabled because she felt that such identification was helpful to her and would likely help others deal with their difficulties:

The evening I heard those students tell their own stories, it was good to know someone else has gone through hell, too. And then to see other people who've gone through college, and to know it's possible for me to go on to college and actually get by. That's the reason I speak as part of the LD support group.

Some students said that telling others about their learning disability often had very positive social consequences: One student claimed that his disability was an advantage in attracting women, because "girls love stuff like that, things refracting in weird ways." He also felt that his disability made him unique and intriguing:

It can be funny. I love to be offbeat, a little bit different. When I tell people I'm learning disabled, I can see people look at me and think, "What is he? He's a little offbeat. He's a slow beat or a beat behind." Some would say a little creative or kind of peculiar.

Another individual recalled that his learning disability had prompted his college newspaper to do a front page story about him. Afterward, he became very well known on campus. He explained, however, that he was careful to phrase his problem in a way that was minimally stigmatizing, noting that "learning disability was a dirty word, so I was dyslexic, which was much cooler."

A young woman believed that telling others about her learning disability had improved her character. Reportedly, it had helped her "stand up for herself, and be seen by others as strong." Further, she noted that telling others has "enhanced me socially and made me more outgoing and verbal. Because of my LD I've become a hard worker, and people respect me."

I don't say anything. Several people stated that they avoided divulging their learning disabilities to all but those they absolutely had to. One young woman, for example, declared that her roommate knew, but that "I never told anybody. Not even my closest friends knew. They just thought I was a studious person, and I decided to leave it at that."

Another individual had a variety of reasons for concealment, including some that reportedly emanated from institutional representatives who were concerned that his accommodations might be interpreted by other students as special treatment:

Other than to my immediate family, and to one other law student who was a friend of mine, I didn't mention it [my LD] to anyone, because it's just one of those things that is difficult to mention to people, and since I functioned so well generally without anyone knowing about my problem, there was no reason to bring it up. I also kept it quiet because the associate dean requested it, realizing that some people would be suspicious. It was a complicated situation for me. Trying to explain it to anyone, especially in a competitive situation, would have been difficult, so I kept it to myself. When I do let friends know, they have a lot of trouble believing it, because all my friends have seen me as a good student, and they couldn't understand what my learning disability could be.

Some persons decided not to tell others about their disability, even though they knew others around them were having similar problems. One individual knew that four or five of his fraternity brothers were experiencing academic difficulties. However, he did not know why, and owing to the unsatisfactory response he got when he had divulged his learning disability to others, he was not about to volunteer any such information about himself. He related that "when I said I have a learning disability, nobody said anything. I don't know how they feel about it, so I don't say anything. I'm just like anybody else here [at college]." A young woman reported that on two occasions men she was dating had terminated the relationship when they found out about her disability. Summarizing her present approach, she said:

If I'm honest about my learning disability, I get avoidance from men who are uncomfortable with it. Now I have this phobia about sharing the truth with people in whom I am interested. You don't mind the single blows, but when the blows keep coming repeatedly, one after another, it becomes self-diminishing, and it becomes hard to pull one's self-esteem back together for the next battle.

People find out anyway. Despite a large student population, varied schedules, and significant efforts to conceal their disability, individuals reported that those around them somehow found out about their disability. Some persons concluded that the amount of studying they had to do gave them away. As one young woman pointed out:

People find out. It's impossible to hide anything around here. I guess they found out just by asking where I was, and someone saying I'm with my tutor or I'm in the library studying. Someone may ask if I want to go out tonight, and I'll tell them I have a test and can't go. They'll ask when the test is, and I'll say, next week. They get the message and ask someone from my home town why I study so much. That's when someone will tell them I have a learning disability.

In one instance a young woman's need to study under very controlled conditions gave her away, until she was able to alter her physical environment:

> People saw me as being different. When I first got here [to college], I couldn't study with other people in the room. If I'm studying and someone breaks my concentration, I start crying, and people can't understand. I say that you broke my concentration. It's like you broke my Ming vase. Now I have a single room, and I can shut my door and be left alone. The girls on the floor are very receptive to it; they were nice about it.

One student noted that excessive studying may have taken over his life and precluded him from pursuing a normal college existence. He described himself as "obsessed with studying," remarking that he spent every weekend studying. Recently, he broke up with his girlfriend after 3 years. He explained that "sometimes I get my priorities mixed up and put off attention that people need. I should do that. I had a girlfriend, and I guess my priorities were studying over seeing her."

Another person believed that everything she did required an inordinate amount of time, leaving little time for a normal social life. She related that "the time most people spend socializing, I have to spend doing or redoing things that should have been done, like figuring out bank accounts, or writing down appointments, or trying to remember appointments. So I don't have the amount of free time that everyone else has."

Interestingly, one individual related that studying not only affected his social life, but also served as a way to escape from a lack of a social life:

> I don't go out much. I have only gone out twice this semester, because I'm always studying and typing. I wish I had a better social life. Basically, I don't know a lot of people at this school. I guess now I try to keep busy studying so I don't get a chance to think about what's going on. I'm a hard worker, and I'm not worried about achieving success, but I only wish I had someone to share it with.

Several students observed that in a large college many people studied hard without attracting much attention, especially if they achieved good grades. More attention was directed toward people who studied hard yet still achieved poor or mediocre grades. One student said, "Most of my friends know about my learning disability because they see me putting a lot of time into studying and not doing so well."

Controlling information about themselves was also difficult because of other indicators, both inside and outside the classroom. These "giveaways" revealed people as different. Several individuals had to explain accommodative equipment such as tape recorders or the information sheet they were required to give instructors in order to receive accommodations. Several others, working in campus jobs, had to contend with having misspelled signs they had posted within the college's dormitories. One person, who couldn't distinguish right from left, was unable to follow verbal directions.

Managing the Social Consequences

Throughout this chapter people have discussed the various social situations they encountered in the course of their daily activities. As individuals matured, they acquired an array of fairly sophisticated social strategies for managing the people and circumstances around them. One of the subtle, mature strategies people adopted was the use of humor to deflect potentially embarrassing situations. One young man described how he used humor to put his friends at ease:

> Sometimes, if it does bother me, I'll make a joke out of it, maybe to show people it doesn't bother me. Some people feel it's okay to kid me about it; some people feel funny about it. I don't want them to feel bad or sorry for me, so I just make a joke out of it. When I tell some people I'm dyslexic, they'll ask if I see backwards or something, I'll tell them, "Yeah, right now I'm looking at you and your feet are by your head, and your head is on the ground," and they believe me.

Another person described driving situations in which he confused right and left turns, thus incurring the teasing of his friends, who called him dyslexic. He explained that such teasing was welcome, saying, "We joke about it. I'll tell anyone who wants to know about my dyslexia." One individual remembered being appointed his fraternity's social chairman and telling his friends that for the next party he was going "to arrange everything backwards so everything would be good for me." A young man described some experiences he had had as a dormitory supervisor, and how he had turned potentially embarrassing moments into humorous social situations:

> I was an RA and had to write dorm signs telling the residents what's coming up and stuff. There were people who took extreme pleasure in correcting my posters on the board. And I'd say, "You guys know I have a campus brainless contest going on, and whoever comes closest to counting all the misspelled words will win a prize." Actually, if somebody wants to know and is truly interested, I will sit down and tell them I'm learning disabled. Otherwise I'll just come up with cute things like that.

In contrast to those who used humor, many students mentioned that the comments and inquiries of others were often too tiresome, humiliating, and frequent for humor. In most cases people chose to "bite their tongue." Several reportedly used sarcasm to make their point. One person replied to invasive questions about his learning disability by saying that "the doctor dropped me at birth, or my father used to play with the soft spot in my head. So people leave you alone."

Another individual who served as a dormitory supervisor took a directive approach to the reactions of people around her:

> The one problem that I do have is sign making. No matter what I do—use the dictionary or be very slow about writing—I will always misspell. One time when I was an RA and it was Parents' Weekend, I put a bunch of signs around the dorm. I got a note on my door saying: "Your bulletin board is misspelled." I can't recognize my misspellings, so I missed it. Half the parents had already seen it. All I can remember was this scandalizing little note. I was very embarrassed. People always left little notes after that, pointing out my misspellings. This year I approached it differently. I said right off that I couldn't spell. I explained to people that I will forget an E and that for them to just put the letters in if I forget them and be a little less direct about my mistakes. They can point out the mistakes, and I'll make the correction and put the sign back up. But don't put scandalizing little notes on it, because that embarrasses me. They all kind of laughed about it, and it's become like a game to see who can find my mistakes first.

Despite the use of varied and sophisticated social strategies, some college students mentioned that they still harbored social anxieties that dictated their behavior with others. Some said they shied away from games that involved counting, spelling, or calculating. One individual cited her reluctance to drive with friends to unknown areas because of her difficulty with directions.

Many people indicated that their learning disability did not prevent them from making friends or becoming involved in social activities. Several, however, mentioned inhibitions about participating *actively* in group activities. One individual reported becoming quiet and withdrawn in groups where he did not know everyone. Another person stated that he "didn't have a great vocabulary, and wasn't always sure he was using the right words." He remarked: "When people are listening to me, sometimes they'll look at me funny and I'll think, 'Oh, my God, I said the wrong word.' So I don't use big words."

SUMMARY

Although learning disabilities, in contrast to other forms of disability, have been termed "invisible," the social effects of being labeled and treated as learning disabled were reported as anything but invisible. Such effects included not only others' responses to people's academic problems, but also their responses to the stigmatizing consequences of the label.

Most people in the study were not formally labeled until they had been in school for at least a few years. Before being formally classified, some had to contend with the stigma of being unable to read or spell, or of getting poor grades. Some persons reported that getting poor grades could be stigmatizing, particularly if their friends were middle- and upper-class, college-aspiring students, and/or if their poor performance was highlighted, even inadvertently, by their teachers. However, many stated that good friends usually did not reject them just because of their academic problems. In fact, along with families, friends were often cited as great sources of support. Students also noted that bad grades were not unusual and could be attributed to a variety or combination of factors—school, personality, teacher, and/or individual motivation—none of which was necessarily stigmatizing.

Being classified as learning disabled did not often or appreciably improve one's grades; furthermore, and more importantly, it led to special class placements away from friends and with students who were publicly certified as deficient. This placement was viewed as more socially stigmatizing than bad grades because it was very visible, more difficult to explain away, and more physically and socially isolating. Thus, it was institutional responses to bad grades, more than the bad grades themselves, that required the development of sophisticated social management strategies.

It was also observed that individuals changed such strategies as the situation and setting changed, and as they modified their views of the problem. This is well illustrated in people's relations with peers, instructors, and employers, where candor and camouflage varied as people learned more about the setting, tasks, and people around them and developed more sophisticated management strategies.

It did not appear that a person's social functioning was negatively affected by his or her learning difficulties. Most individuals studied seemed very socially involved in many school and extraschool activities. In fact, well-developed social skills and heightened involvement in nonacademic activities were primary avenues for demonstrating competence, reducing the effects of the label, compensating for poor academic performance, and gaining peer acceptance. Thus, many persons demonstrated varied, sophisticated, and well-used social skills.

Students also mentioned the need to talk their way in and out of situations with peers and teachers, and to manipulate social circumstances to their advantage by camouflaging their problems or deflecting other's attention through humor. Thus, their successful adaptation to various social, educational, and vocational situations actually depended on their social abilities.

A relatively small percentage of persons elected to hide their learning disability label from everyone they could. Others found their disability to be at worst nothing to hide and at best a distinct social advantage whereby they seemed more intriguing to others. Most people, however, adopted social strategies somewhere between these two approaches, telling their close friends and those who seemed trustworthy. They also employed strategies for mitigating any possible negative social consequences. For example, in elementary and high school, students tried to "fake it," giving the impression they did not care; or to excel in some extracurricular or extraschool activity. College students more often used humor and direct education with their peers.

Retention of privacy was an important objective for many persons because the selection of particular social strategies often depended on their ability to control information about themselves. For elementary and high school students, privacy was virtually impossible to control. Even in seemingly anonymous settings such as college, students noted the difficulty of keeping their label private. Often the use of formal accommodations, such as tutorial assistance, extra time on tests, and tape recorders in class, gave them away. Also, it was difficult to conceal anything from roommates. Even those who tried to conceal their disability from everyone could not successfully hide it from those with whom they lived. Students were also discovered because they had to study harder and with less success than their peers, and/or because they participated in special study groups or received special services. Most persons did not want their friends to think that their extensive studying, academic problems, and special treatment were due to "stupidity," so many voluntarily disclosed their label to those around them. Some individuals in the study experienced or anticipated social rejection. As was noted previously, many concluded that their learning disability was stigmatizing and therefore something to hide, obscure, or reveal only to trusted friends. Thus, at least some of the isolation reported by people was not due either to social skills deficits or to learning disability pathology (for a discussion of hypotheses of social skills deficits see Gresham, 1988), but to a social caution pursued in relations with others. Such caution was, in fact, a method of managing social relationships and difficult social situations.

Some people, because of the time they spent organizing themselves for work and/or school, had little time for a full social life and many friends. These individuals still relished their social activities, although they reportedly socialized less frequently than their friends and believed that they participated in fewer social groups. Overall, there was little evidence that the young adults with learning disabilities in this study participated in fewer social activities because of social inadequacies. In many cases their restricted social functioning was voluntary, and reflected a lack of time rather than a dearth of skills.

5

Managing the Workplace

Only 22 of the 49 individuals interviewed had what was termed a substantial employment history. This meant that they were working, or had worked, full-time at one job for at least 3 consecutive months, or had been employed for a minimum of 1 year at a variety of part-time jobs. The remaining people had only short-term or sporadic employment experience, mostly because they were students. In a few cases people reported having difficulty finding and maintaining even short-term jobs.

The bulk of this section deals with the more experienced workers, although there are occasional references to those with limited employment experiences. Table 5.1 lists the types of jobs held by each of the individuals with substantive work experience.

EMPLOYMENT PROSPECTS

Work as a Source of Anxiety

Individuals expressed disparate views of their employment prospects. Some individuals, even those who had substantial work histories and those who had successfully mastered college and graduate school, were very worried about entering the work world. Most of them perceived the employment arena as very different from their college settings. They wondered if their deficiencies would be tolerated, and they worried whether they could handle the demands placed on them. For one individual, school seemed a comfortable and familiar place compared to the employment world:

> My biggest worry is the transference from the nice, cozy environment of college to the real world. That's pretty scary. I wonder if I'll have anything to stand on if someone fires me? I spent a lot of time and money getting ready for a career that I really can do, but that one little part of it [writing] is always brought up. In fact, last night I

Table 5.1 Employment Duration and Experiences of Persons
With Substantial Employment

SUBJECT	OCCUPATION(S)	APPROXIMATE DURATION
1.	Caseworker	6 months
2.	Payroll clerk, secretary, shoe salesperson	1 year
3.	Nurse	3 years
4.	Lawyer	6 months
5.	Bank teller	3 months
6.	Watch salesperson, computer salesperson	6 months
7.	Bakery worker, nursery worker, ecology instructor	3 years
8.	Mental health worker, computer specialist	3 years
9.	Preschool teacher	1 year
10.	Computer programmer	1 year
11.	Owner of small business	1 year
12.	Cook, parking attendant, manual laborer, machine repairperson	4–5 years
13.	Graphic artist	9 months
14.	Director of counseling at social service agency	2 years
15.	File clerk in military service, supervisor in legal office, meat delivery person	10 years
16.	Car mechanic, auto parts inventory clerk, industrial supply clerk	4½ years
17.	Bookkeeper/secretary in family business	10 years
18.	Cook, civil engineering assistant	1 year
19.	Electronic hardware salesperson	1½ years
20.	Salesperson (clothing store)	2 years
21.	Graphic artist, printing technician	2 years
22.	Chemical worker	7 months

couldn't sleep because I was thinking about that. It looks good now but you don't know. I know that there have been a lot of people who have had this problem and have made it; sometimes I wonder how.

Not being able to complete assignments on time was a source of anxiety for many persons entering or reentering the work world. In college this was a major problem, which was often ameliorated by the use of time extensions. However, several persons still worried that failure to meet deadlines would emerge as a major obstacle in the workplace:

You know I survived school. I thought that was the big hurdle. But it turns out it isn't. I was good at school. I could go back. But I really don't see that I'm ever going to eliminate the fact that I take twice as long to do things as other people.

A person with an extensive and successful work history in the military was very worried about his chances of succeeding in civilian arenas:

In the military when you're a sergeant you can order someone to do a job. Even if it was my job, people do it. In the civilian world if you try to tell someone else to do your work, they'll tell you to go fly a kite. I'm worried a lot about whether I can make it. In the military I found ways around my bad writing and spelling. In school I'm trying to improve on my weaknesses, which is hard. But even though I got a degree, if I was a boss and I had a choice of two different people with degrees and one can spell 100% better than the other, I would hire the guy who could spell, right? So that really bothers me.

Work as an Opportunity

Not everyone saw the employment arena as hostile. Some people saw it as an escape from their learning disability. One person, who used minimal formal accommodations during his education, and who had begun a business while attending college, bemoaned the lack of respect and recognition he was accorded in school:

One of the biggest frustrations I had was, I saw how good I was in the outside world, and how my friends and family looked at me. On the outside I was looked up to and respected. And then I'd cross the line into school and I'd be really struggling for everything I could get. It's tough being in both worlds because I don't struggle in the outside world, I flow. But sometimes I think, "Oh, my God, I'm going to fail and never get to the outside world." But out there no one has ever asked me for my grade point average.

Another person related that school was the only place where he had felt that he had a learning disability:

In college I had always had trouble getting enough information out of my head and writing it onto the paper. Possibly, if I had never gone to law school, I'd never have been diagnosed as learning disabled. Really, the learning disability didn't seem to affect me until I got to law school, and I suspect that it isn't going to affect me now that I'm working [as a lawyer]. I did a lot of sales work and I never had any conception at all that I had any learning disability. And now that I'm working in the law, I don't have any real feeling that I'm learning disabled.

A man was unable to earn a degree but rose from caseworker in a small group home to casework supervisor in a large social service organization. He described the psychological frustrations he encountered in school:

College is another thing. I've never graduated. As a matter of fact, I'm the only nondegree person here at [the agency] that has a supervisory position. I'm the only nondegree counselor here. But I can't read and write and pass the tests unless the professor works on short answer, group participation, or verbal interaction. Then I could do quite well. I used to take courses knowing that I'd never pass. But I went for the education and felt very frustrated believing that I knew some of that material but not getting credit for it. I just knew I couldn't pass it, and I bolted on so many courses and ended up taking incompletes when I really knew the material.

GETTING A JOB

Telling Employers Early

A major dilemma for persons seeking employment was how to approach employers about their learning disability. Some believed that they should tell employers about their disability as early as possible. Most people advocating this position tended to have less work experience. One young woman studying to be a nurse felt that an employer had a right to know about her learning disability. She also believed that it was an advantage that an employer knew "right away what I had." She explained further that:

> It [telling them] helps them understand why it takes me longer to understand the procedures. It allows the person the chance to know the employers, and if they are going to be prejudiced or get mad at you. That's an unhealthy situation, and I wouldn't want to work there.

Another person believed that telling employers right away was a way of protecting himself in case he could not do the job:

> Don't cover it. Don't hide it. It's always going to be on my [job] applications. It's always in my records, and I'm not afraid to tell employers. What happens if you cover it and you get the job and can't handle it? You've got to say, I've got this learning problem, and if he decides to overlook it, great. You might as well tell him up front instead of getting canned right away because you can't handle the job.

One person reasoned that hiding her learning disability might give the wrong impression:

> Since my learning disability is not that severe, it might look like I was trying to cover it up, which is really silly. I'm not [trying to cover it up], and I never would. There's nothing wrong with having it. It's something I was born with. That's the way I am, and if they don't like it, tough.

Only a few experienced workers advocated telling employers about their learning disability initially. One young woman did so, but related that the information did little to increase the assistance she received from her supervisors:

> Before I accepted the position I told him point-blank that I was learning disabled. I wanted him to know so that there would be no question about it if I had a difficult time integrating information. That gave me someone who knew I had a learning disability and still

wanted me to work for him. I also shared with my supervisor, peers, and people around work that I had a learning disability, and that was why it was taking me so long to integrate information. I told the director that I had some special needs, but he didn't want to spend too much time discussing things, and it took time to explain things. There are limited accommodations, and there is need for a lot of growth on the part of both the director and my supervisor. My supervisor doesn't have the knowledge, coping skills, or—most of all—the patience to deal with this.

Not Telling Employers

The majority of people interviewed leaned toward withholding information on their initial contacts with employers. Reportedly, they did so because they believed that (a) the disability was none of the employer's business; (b) most employers did not know what a learning disability was, anyway; (c) the information might be held against them; (d) the disability might not affect their work performance; and (e) it was likely that nothing could be done about their problems anyway.

Some individuals were opposed to telling employers anything. One young woman, for example, argued that telling an employer early might hurt her chances of getting and keeping a job:

Employers, when dealing with the handicapped, may not hire you because of ignorance. They figure, "How are you going to make it in this office?" Why tell them? It's just important that I know, and how I choose to deal with it. They're not going to give me any special benefits because I'm special. I'm not going to get a pay raise or a pat on the back. I fit in just fine the way I am without telling them anything. And if I don't tell them, they won't see me as any different. Since you can't see that I'm disabled, you don't have to know.

The majority of people concluded that the best strategy for revealing their disability to employers was to wait until they "got to know their boss," had established a solid work record, or had encountered difficulties in carrying out their duties. One individual believed that the label might be misunderstood at first, but believed he would reveal it if he ran into problems with the job:

I don't think I would. No, definitely, I wouldn't put it on an application. Maybe after I got the job and was having difficulty with something, I would say, "Look, I've got this little problem; it's not really major." When you say "learning disability" people really look at you. They don't really understand what it means.

Another person also believed she would not reveal her disability initially unless absolutely necessary, and she would be cautious about divulging information even after she had established herself as a good employee:

> I wouldn't tell right away unless it involved something that I would definitely need to compensate for. But I think I can compensate for myself quite well now, so I don't think I will tell. But down the line, once they gain my trust, and see that I'm a strong worker, and have no reason to let me go, I might let it slip. But if I think it's a fact that may get me fired, I'd keep my mouth shut. That's none of their business, and that's the attitude I'll take. I won't apply that way, but if I find myself in a tough situation, I have no problem telling someone.

Several persons who did not reveal their disability right away to employers did, however, provide hints about their problems during initial interviews. Individuals recalled telling employers that they had trouble spelling, or that they "were not fast but thorough." Several individuals decided to camouflage what they felt were their most serious, or general, flaws behind less serious, more specific, difficulties. One person, for example, noted:

> In the first interview I might tell them I can't spell, because some time they may wonder if I can do typesetting. I'm completely unqualified to do typesetting, so I'm not afraid to say that. But I am afraid to say that I have trouble understanding directions because that will turn everybody off.

Some people with substantial employment histories opted to tell employers of their learning disabilities in the initial interview. All but one of those who did so said that they would not make the same decision again. Two persons were eventually fired, although neither of them believed their dismissal had occurred because of their disability. They did feel, however, that revealing such information early in the hiring process offered them few advantages, if any. In one of these situations a woman was confused as to why she was fired as a bank teller, recalling that she had received little assistance when she had encountered early difficulties:

I told them at my job interview I am dyslexic. They said they didn't know anything about it and what does it mean? I sat and talked to the lady about it [the learning disability] for a while, and then she said, "Well, I hope you can handle it." I had a difficult time with 2 weeks of job training. When I finished, I had a lot of shortages and none of the people would help me find them, so it was difficult. I don't know why I got fired. They said because I had too many shortages, but I know for a fact that it had to be more than that; my supervisor or the manager didn't like me. I don't think that those shortages had anything to do with my dyslexia. My dad says yes, but I don't think so.

Another individual, fired as a counselor at a community residence, remembered informing his supervisor about his learning disability and being told, "No problem. Don't worry about it." When the young man was unable to compensate for his writing weakness or to record intelligible case notes at the end of the day, he was fired. He described the situation:

Most jobs are set up for people who write well, and I don't write well. They didn't like the way I wrote in the log. They couldn't read my writing because my spelling is so bad. I couldn't use my dictation equipment because there was no one there to transcribe it, and the log needed to be filled out right when I went off duty. So I didn't write much, and I think they thought I was lazy because I wasn't writing much. Sometimes they would say, "Look what he wrote," and tell me to take more time.

A woman who was required to tell her employer right away about her disability to be eligible for special employment consideration said that she would not reveal her disability in future job applications. Her employer had provided accommodations and was satisfied with her work. However, she found out from her supervisor that her position was known throughout the company as the one for a disabled person, a situation that violated her privacy and was stigmatizing. During her first week on the job she became self-conscious, wondering whether co-workers were asking each other: "Is she disabled? What's the matter with her? Is she deaf?" From this experience she developed strategies for researching where to apply and whether or not to reveal her disability:

I have a hard and fast rule that I'm not going to tell employers [about the disability]. The form says it has to be a disability that prevents you from doing the job; so all I have to do is decide that it doesn't prevent me from doing the job, and then I don't have to say anything. I can fake it. I'll also be careful where I apply. I'll look into where I apply maybe a little more carefully than someone else. I'll look at how they handle other strange things, like minority hiring, paternity leave, special programs for certain people. If you find companies that do those things, they seem to be a good flexible company, and recognize that people are different.

This caution was consistent with the advice of a social services supervisor who was learning disabled but also did a lot of hiring. This man neither revealed his disability when he sought work nor believed it was wise for other job seekers to reveal their learning disability to him:

People who tell employers had better be good at what they do. This sounds like real prejudice, but I might not hire the person, because the bottom line is that reading and writing is important. We just don't have the skills that other people have, and you're going to have to overcompensate. There are so many people who can handle that job, and employers aren't going to accommodate you. You're there to accommodate them, and people need to be prepared for that. You have to prove you have something real special that they want.

Maybe there are certain fields they [persons with learning disabilities] shouldn't be in. In many cases I know I didn't help people as much as I could have if I had been able to read and write properly. I also know about the lack of communication which can result [from having learning disabilities].

Confusion and Ambivalence

Not all those interviewed were sure about what they would tell prospective employers. Many were confused and ambivalent:

I don't know if I'd tell them right off. I'd have to see. I don't see why not. I don't know if it would help me or hurt me. It's just that if you get a job and mess up, the boss thinks you don't know what you're doing. If you tell him straight out that you have a problem, maybe he'll help you out.

Another individual wondered about the effects of the information on an employer even after being hired:

I really wonder if I should tell them. If I tell them at the initial interview, and they know anything about it—I mean, what would you think? That's a strong question. I don't know, I might go through the interview, and if they hire me I'll explain to them that I have dyslexia. I was told that they couldn't fire me then, and that they'd have to give me accommodations, but I really wonder if I should tell them at all.

KEEPING A JOB

The majority of people elected not to tell employers about their learning disability until after they had been employed for awhile. They relied at first on informal accommodations to succeed vocationally. Many of these persons, however, anticipated eventually obtaining formal accommodations. Several persons said that early in their careers they had anticipated receiving assistive devices such as a personal computer, and/or job modifications such as being given a secretary, a reader, and/or specific techniques for circumventing their deficiencies. However, none of the experienced workers actually received any formal accommodations. All of them reportedly relied on arrangements made on their own without the formal participation or support of the employer. The two most prevalent arrangements people emphasized were (a) reorganizing their surroundings, and (b) getting help.

Organizing the Work Setting

Becoming organized was manifested in numerous ways. Most frequently it entailed covertly rearranging the work requirements and setting in ways that made the job manageable. In most cases this involved doing the job differently than it had been done before and concealing that difference from a supervisor or boss. Getting organized could involve such simple procedures as making "memory cards" to remember instructions, spellings, names, and locations. Organizing one's setting could also include complex functions such as changing the way people in an office related to each other and did their jobs.

A lawyer with a learning disability reported that when he began his career, he had experienced problems doing the required written work, especially when he was under pressure. He had anticipated the problem and, during the initial job interview, had emphasized his thoroughness rather than his speed. After being hired, he avoided writing as much as possible by dictating his work, and unlike his predecessors and co-workers, did almost all of his work by phone rather than letter.

A man who was hired to conduct children's ecology tours developed a specific system for improving his performance:

> In my job introducing grade school children to woodland ecology, I found it very hard to communicate with the students in terms of getting the knowledge across and organizing it nicely during the walk through the forest. I knew how much better I should be, and that made me not want to do the job. I felt uncomfortable. I developed little strategies. I used little notecards and tried to draw little pictures which would help me remember what I was going to say and demonstrating what I was going to do. The note cards and the pictures helped. A couple of years ago I wasn't too good at realizing I had this problem, and I ought to spend more time thinking about what I can do to improve it. I wasn't really thinking in those terms.

Another young man remembered finally getting up the nerve to seek a paramedic job he had always wanted but was afraid to apply for because of its writing requirements. After making some initial spelling mistakes, he developed some self-made adaptive devices to help him overcome his spelling problems:

> After I made a few spelling mistakes, I told them I had dyslexia. The person in charge of the training division understood the problem and was able to explain it to the rest of the management. They have been helpful in working with it. But one of the things I did for myself was I made up what they call cheat sheets. I have a list of words that I use most commonly. It's all medical terminology, and if I feel that I'm spelling a word wrong or don't know how to spell it, I just go to this sheet. I wrapped the sheet in plastic and carry it around with me.

For one person, job success often depended on "how fast I can organize the job and me." Getting organized also meant learning how to concentrate and reduce the stress of the job:

> When I get a new job the first thing I have to do is to get real organized real fast. How well I can cope with a job depends on how chaotic the situation is. If I can get the chaos out, I can handle the

job as well as anybody, but I can't just wade into it and do it off the cuff as well as another person might. Once I got a job as a stripper/platemaker/camera person in a print shop. I'd have these job orders that would come in over the phone from the boss, scrawled on a job order or on the original. It wasn't coming in the same form, and it was terrifying to try and put this stuff together. I was just dreaming about it all night. I came pretty close to losing my job just through forgetting things and missing phone numbers. I found I had to have time to get into a job and make a pattern out of it. I had to concentrate my attention on what was going on and not lose that concentration. I found that I got better at establishing a way to handle information. My mental organization got better. I found out when things get tough, I tune out like a fantasy, and that's something I have to fight. I think I've managed to concentrate better in business and job-oriented situations.

To keep his position, a sergeant in the military found a way to reorganize ths entire office structure and staff. He depended on deceit, manipulation, and organization:

After I had an accident, they put me in an office and said I had to be a file clerk. I liked sitting in the office because it was easy. Then they asked me if I could type and I said, "Yeah, I can do all this work." So they said I could work in the legal office. And I went from legal clerk inside of 6 months to the legal chief, and within a year to a legal officer. That's because I had people under me with less rank and I had them doing their work and, without them knowing it, had manipulated them into doing my work. There wasn't really that much work to do, but I asked for another man. So basically I had the two regular staff plus an extra man who kind of carried my load. All I had to do was sign what they had done and spend a lot of time looking at books so they thought I was doing work.

I was always afraid I was going to be found out. Like one time I had to do an Article 15 hearing, which is like a court-martial, because my staff was not there. At the hearing I usually had one of my men take notes. But this time I had to take the notes myself, and I knew I couldn't do it. At the real court-martials they taped the hearings, so I decided to tape the Article 15 hearings. When I brought the tape recorder in, the CO [commanding officer] said, "What's this? You have to take notes." I said that since they taped at the court-martials we should follow their lead and do it here, too. He thought that was a good idea. They thought I was doing a great job and would put me up for meritorious promotion. At that point, the way I had the office set up, the CO thought I was irreplaceable.

Several people with reading and writing problems described how they had circumvented their difficulties and successfully carried out their jobs. One individual, a cook on a houseboat, was expected to read recipe books and develop menus for a work crew of 30 men. He had to find his own resource materials and adapt them to the situation:

> Coming from a family of 11, I knew how to boil water, and I knew how to look into a recipe book and at least come up with an idea. If I couldn't find stroganoff in the cookbook, I'd buy one with pictures and look for things I recognized. I never used just one recipe so I would cross-reference off of one book to another. I also don't cook by the book, but by how things look like they belong together. So I got by with little reading.

A social worker who reported poor writing and spelling skills had to record the day's events at the end of his shift in a facility for disturbed youth. He used a variety of creative strategies and adaptive equipment to succeed:

> Many times I would have the person I was replacing write down the log. I would dictate the log to him and say that this was better staff communication, which it was. And I used a tape recorder to a degree, even though it wasn't as helpful as the dictating. One of my biggest problems was remembering and writing the many phone messages and appointments I have. So I used the tape recorder for taking notes and remembering things I had to do.
>
> I also was organized to never put anything off, because unless I followed through right away while it was in my mind, I'd forget it. So if I had something I could take care of in the building, I would get off the phone and walk down to the person or department and take care of the task and come back. I got things done when they needed to be, but it didn't help my relations with co-workers. Other people thought I was pushy and aggressive, but the only way I could get my job done was to do one thing at a time and do it right.

Getting Help

Often, despite their best efforts, persons with learning disabilities could not keep a job by working hard and/or organizing their work settings around their disabilities. They needed additional help, and co-workers were a major source of such assistance. A paramedic, for example, told how his partners would always check his daily reports for spelling and writing mistakes. After being hired, a computer specialist with a writing problem discovered that many "computer types can't write, so my spelling and writing problems were no big deal." He noted that the company managed this problem by organizing much of the work around groups. In this way, persons with writing problems still could contribute creatively. Their writing mistakes would be corrected early by members of the group who could spell and write well. He also found that after a few months on the job, some co-workers volunteered to check his other work, too.

In some cases people felt bad for having to depend on others. As a secretary emphasized, however, such assistance was often crucial:

> I have trouble taking messages correctly. Typing is a problem, speed is a big issue, and doing things under pressure. Someone drops off a manuscript in the morning and say they need it by 4 o'clock. I can't do it. What has happened is that I've gotten the support of the other staff, and they pitch in and help me. That's an imposition on them. I feel terrible about it, but I can't do anything about it. I am very grateful and I express that repeatedly.

A day-care teacher told how her supervisor had discovered her problems and helped her manage her spelling and writing shortcomings:

> I really never planned on telling anyone, but a couple of months into the job, the director noticed that I wasn't spelling words right that I was putting on the daily calendar. In some cases what I wrote didn't make sense. She didn't make a big deal about it; she just corrected it. Finally I decided to explain why I was doing that, so that I didn't appear stupid. After I told her, it didn't change a thing. She asked me afterwards if I wanted her to proofread what I wrote for parent conferences in order to avoid any embarrassment. So I agreed because it would be embarrassing if a parent thought a teacher can't even write properly.

Several individuals reported that their job situations changed, and that what had appeared at first to be a manageable job turned into a position requiring assistance. A social work supervisor had begun as a counselor who was confident and competent. When asked to assume the supervisory position, however, he had to do more case management and began to struggle and lose his confidence:

> It wasn't working out. I was getting ready to quit and went to my supervisor and told him that I couldn't keep up with the job. Then he told me that they wanted me to stay even if I didn't write another thing while I was there. He then offered to help me in any way he could to improve my skills. I'll never forget that. It was a highlight of my life.

In a different situation, a woman working in a printing company found that the help she had received in one department was not available in another. In the first setting, her poor spelling and letter reversals were evident but were not damaging because there were proofreaders available to check her work. Her supervisor also liked her, "was very understanding, and would double check for any errors." When she was promoted to a better-paying job in another department, however, the job changed a little, and the assistance she had received from co-workers was no longer available:

> I took a job in which I had to answer the phone and take messages, and I couldn't do it. Also, you had to do your own proofreading, and I wasn't able to handle it. I always thought I was a unique designer, but in the business world I was exposed to answering phones, reading, and co-workers wondering why I couldn't proofread. Then one day they were trying to meet a deadline and I was making up an ad and messed up the phone number. The boss really yelled at me, and finally they let me go. I looked for work. People liked my portfolio. I have a lot of talent and creativity, but there is no job. So I just kind of gave up. Then I got married, but I don't know what to do. There doesn't seem to be a job for me out there.

In some circumstances people relied on family members to assist them with their jobs. One individual recalled how his wife helped him cover up his deficiencies in his military job:

> When I first went in I was covering up and doing a lot of running around. Once I got married I was able to get more stuff done and get promoted faster. In order to get promoted I had to do my job great and get a meritorious promotion. To get a regular promotion you had to know the books and go in front of a board and answer questions. So I spent a lot of time doing my job, putting in that extra

effort so I would get promoted. Before I got married I probably spent 10 or 12 hours, where most people were spending 8 hours a day. One time I had to review a lot of records, and my wife and I went down to the office in the evening when everyone was gone, and she helped me go through all the record books. She helped me because she didn't want me losing my job either.

GETTING FIRED

Eight individuals with substantial employment experience each reported being fired from at least one job. When people discussed being fired, they inevitably focused on specific failings that they felt had led to their dismissal, and attributed these failings to their learning disabilities. For example, one person, fired from his job as a salesman, related:

I went into the supply business, where there was a lot of room for advancement, but my disability got in the way of a whole lot. I started out in the warehouse putting supplies away, and sometimes they'd have a parts number that was maybe 20 characters long. I was a good worker but I made a lot of mistakes. With 20 characters there was a lot of chance for error. Then I went to inside sales, but again I had to write up bills, spell customers' names. I'd make spelling errors that didn't look very good, and I was let go.

Another person described his failure as a delivery man:

I was a delivery man for a meat company, and I messed up some orders. He [the supervisor] said if I did it again, he'd let me go. I had to read the orders to know what to load on the truck. I couldn't read the orders and understand them. They'd write something like they needed seven chickens, and I'd understand that. But then he'd add on two more and make a quick plus sign with a 2 next to it. He would write it close together and I wouldn't understand it and mess up the orders.

One man briefly described two unsuccessful job situations:

I've been fired from a lot of crummy jobs. I worked as a cook and it was hell to keep track of the orders in my head and not screw them up. I had a job mixing chemicals in a motion picture film processing

plant, and got fired because I couldn't keep the chemicals straight.
I'd either skip one or put twice as much [as] I needed of another.

Reading and writing tasks, spelling requirements, and duties that
had to be understood and carried out quickly, accurately, and sometimes under pressure were reported as particularly troublesome by
those interviewed. It is noteworthy, however, that the preceding failures did not always, or consistently, lead to being fired. Many people
who reported having similar deficiencies and experiences as those who
were fired described successful employment adjustments. One, for
example, reported having difficulty recording customer orders and
names but found a way around it:

> I owned a greenhouse and a nursery and had some problems
> communicating with customers and dealing with the public. I'd
> have to write up orders for weddings and things, and talking with
> people I'd have good ideas, but spelling names and the stupid
> flowers, I couldn't do it. I just couldn't present them with a copy
> because they'd think I wasn't competent or something. So I'd say
> that I'd mail the copy to them. Then I'd go to someone and ask
> them how to spell these things, and they'd help me. It's important
> to realize what you have to do to get around things. Sometimes you
> can do it yourself and sometimes you can't.

In two situations described earlier in the chapter, people working
in group homes were required to record the events of the day in a daily
log. Neither person could do the task, because they couldn't spell, and
no one could read their case notes. Only one of the employees was
fired, however, for this deficiency. The person who was retained had
successfully convinced his co-workers to allow him to dictate his notes
to them.

SUMMARY

Most people labeled learning disabled described employment
situations as more varied, unpredictable, and ambiguous than the
educational settings they had experienced. For some the variability
and ambiguity of the vocational world represented liberation from the
unyielding constraints of education, an arena that had only emphasized and exaggerated their weaknesses and minimized their ability to
function successfully. For them the work world allowed more freedom

to circumvent, even negate, their problems by finding the right job, the right boss, or changing the work setting and tasks to suit them.

For others the work world presented a deeply discouraging place in which people sometimes gave up looking for all but unchallenging jobs, which they knew they could perform. For many interviewees work represented a formidable departure from the more predictable, structured educational settings they had become accustomed to. They described the employment arena as a world that could not be easily managed through the formal strategies they had learned and employed in previous settings, especially previous educational situations.

Most individuals relied on limited work histories and previous educational experiences as points of reference in approaching and managing new job situations. However, previous work experiences were often short-term, temporary, or summer jobs in which they had performed tasks they knew they could do easily. When they entered jobs they considered career positions, or positions they considered challenging, they were often asked to do unfamiliar tasks. Thus, even persons with employment experience were uncertain as to how their academic problems would affect specific employment situations.

To succeed on a specific job, individuals needed to find the assistance they required, and/or to develop alternative ways to complete required job tasks. For example, a social worker who couldn't write legibly or coherently had to find a way to document the day's events in a log book. A secretary who couldn't remember or accurately record messages and phone numbers had to find acceptable methods of doing this part of her job. The development of these adaptations was the major employment issue confronting persons labeled learning disabled. Some people, especially those with less work experience, were inclined to tell a prospective employer about their disability. This was called the "honest approach," and was reportedly the approach recommended most consistently and frequently by the learning disabilities professionals with whom people consulted.

Persons with more work experiences were less inclined to follow the honest approach. These individuals believed that the learning disabilities label altered the way employers viewed them before and after they had been hired. They were concerned about the social stigma attached to their label, and they implemented a variety of covert job-seeking and job-sustaining strategies. Using these approaches, they attempted to conceal their disability label until after they had established a solid social and working relationship with their boss, or until they ran into problems that threatened their job.

Those individuals who had secured a job reported a variety of strategies for keeping it. Interestingly, the most frequently used strategies—concealing the disability, organizing the environment, and getting help from others—were virtually ignored by professionals as formal strategies. In fact, it appeared that people had learned little of how to survive in employment settings from their school, family, or professional affiliations. Most advisors counseled social candor, remedial instruction, and formal adaptive strategies.

Such strategies demonstrated several failings. First, they did not address very well the social stigma that concerned many individuals and led them to conceal their formal label. Although employers, like teachers and college professors, knew little about learning disabilities, seldom were they under any stringent institutional mandates to accommodate people with learning disabilities, and seldom were they inclined to hire individuals for professional positions whom they felt could be a liability in such crucial areas as reading, writing, and organization. Thus, prospective job applicants felt that they should present themselves carefully and develop a strategy for revealing themselves, both initially as well as later on, if and when they encountered difficulty with aspects of the job. A second failing of most adaptive strategies is that, although presumed applicable to most life settings, they were designed primarily in and for the educational world. Employment settings were widely diverse in structure, demands, predictability, and flexibility, and were not as easily fitted to accommodations such as time extensions and assistive equipment. Educational classes, despite varying course content and instructional methods, shared a common structure that lent itself to a small series of accommodations.

In sum, individuals entering or functioning in the work world found themselves in novel, sometimes ambiguous circumstances, with neither a clearly defined role identity nor any sources of formal support like those that existed in their schools and/or families. Individuals had to rethink and sometimes unlearn the formal social roles and adaptive strategies they had been taught. While informal adaptive strategies reportedly enabled people to succeed in school and work situations, such strategies have not been well acknowledged or described in the field's literature. This appears to be a serious omission, because it was these informal, covert, manipulative activities which people reported as essential elements of their employment successes.

6

Changing the
Learning Disabilities Emphasis

This chapter presents an analysis of people's descriptions of their experiences and discusses how they have interpreted and managed educational, vocational, familial, and social situations. In many cases their descriptions have revealed personal beliefs, social meanings, experiences, relationships, and behaviors that have so far received only marginal professional scrutiny, but which nonetheless reflect important social, psychological, and behavioral realities. These realities seem particularly important for labeled persons and their families wishing to successfully manage their circumstances, and for professionals and policy makers attempting to understand and improve people's lives.

CONSTRUCTING AND APPLYING THE
LEARNING DISABILITIES LABEL

Although the formal societal designation of learning disabilities is physiogenic in nature, a number of extra-individual determinants of the label have been identified. Persons in the study described, for example, the value judgments of those around them and the institutional arrangements in which they participated as important contributors to their learning disabilities designation.

Labeling Proponents and Value Judgments

Many people do poorly in school and are not considered learning disabled (although the numbers of people with this diagnosis have increased so dramatically that some have advocated limiting the percentages of children who may receive the diagnosis). In fact, Algozzine (1985), and Algozzine and Ysseldyke (1985) found very few distinctions between low-achieving students and those classified as learning disabled. From the literature and from people's descriptions in this study, it appears that learning disabilities diagnoses are based on more than intra-individual/physiogenic factors.

Individuals recalled being labeled at different times, for different reasons, by different people, and with different effects. In addition to getting what they considered poor grades, people recalled having a labeling proponent, such as a parent, teacher, or learning disabilities specialist, conclude that he or she "is not measuring up," that "something is wrong" with the person, and that "something should be done." The standards used to determine whether or not people were "measuring up," and whether or not "something was wrong," were based on inferred, rather than direct, neurogenic evidence, and on value judgments that varied from family to family, school to school, professional to professional, even parent to parent.

Whereas learning disabilities have been formally defined as an objectively given, intra-individual disorder of the central nervous system, it appears that physiogenic dysfunction had little to do with most people's classification. Such conclusions coincide with Becker's (1973) conclusion that any episodes of deviance "require the overt or tacit cooperation of many people and groups to occur as they do" (p. 183). Becker argued that the complex circumstances surrounding identified deviance cast doubt on theories that attribute behavior to individual psychology and seek the origins of specified behaviors in mysterious physiogenic forces. "A miraculous meeting of individual forms of pathology would have to be proposed in order to account for the complicated forms of collective activity which have been observed" (Becker, 1973, p. 183).

Learning to be Learning Disabled

More evidence for extra-individual, systemic determinants of learning disabilities may be found in situations where people described having "learned to be learning disabled." That is, conditions and practices within schools, colleges, and families could reinforce, exacerbate, and even create academic and social behaviors later identified as learning disabled. This phenomenon has been termed "learning to be learning disabled," and could occur because of disabling treatment situations, narrow coping strategies, and institutional interests.

Disabling treatment approaches. Reportedly, treatment methods applied to people's academic problems could create "learning disabled" behaviors. It should not be inferred that treatments, in and of themselves, caused learning disabilities. However, the social, professional, and institutional responses to individuals identified as learning disabled placed them in situations that made it harder for them to pursue typical social, educational, and/or vocational relations and routines as pursued by other persons in similar circumstances.

For many learning disabled individuals and their teachers, parents, and peers, the label meant intellectual inferiority, academic incompetence, and disruptive behavior, all of which required special treatment. Following formal classification, people reported being sent to special segregated classes, schools, and colleges. Individuals were also assigned to separate—and what individuals considered socially devalued—organizations for disabled people. Besides the stigmatizing aspects of segregation, special placements separated LD students from their friends, disrupted their daily schedules, and often did not provide the help they needed to progress academically (Biklen & Zollers, 1986; Kavale, 1988; Reynolds & Wang, 1983; Wittrock, 1986). Thus, students were often saddled with both the stigma of special placements and continuing academic problems. It is little wonder that special placements in elementary and high school were frequently and consistently cited as the most aversive consequence of being labeled.

For all of the preceding reasons, people attempted to avoid the label or, failing that, to protect themselves socially and psychologically. Some individuals acted "tough" or indifferent in class. In this way they could claim not to care about school and therefore distinguish themselves from other devalued students who were called "stupid" or "retarded." Pursuing this course of action, they often were dismissed from class, missed classroom material necessary to succeed, and fell further and further behind.

Some individuals "faked it" by trying to hide their problems, and failed to receive academic assistance until it was too late to catch up academically. Whether students "faked it" or acted out in some way, they could set in motion a self-perpetuating cycle of problem behaviors. Delaying or ignoring assistance would worsen and/or create "learning disabled" behaviors because as a result, students fell further behind, thereby demonstrating heightened learning difficulties, reinforcing teacher and parent perceptions of deficiency, creating individual self-doubts, and ultimately leading to academic deficiencies.

Not everyone rejected special assistance. Some families and individuals sought extra help in the form of tutoring or increased instructor assistance. Some students willingly enrolled and remained in special classes, believing that such placements helped them academically.

Even many of these students wished, however, that their special placement could have included persons who wanted academic assistance but were not labeled as disabled.

Narrow adaptive options. Some people argued that the adaptive techniques they had learned from professionals, parents, and teachers in one setting had contributed to their being "learning disabled" in another; college and work situations were the settings most widely cited.

Slightly less than 40% of those in the study were not officially identified as learning disabled until late high school or early college. For these individuals college posed many problems, some of which related to the adaptive methods they learned in school. For example, to succeed in high school some students reportedly opted for easy classes, relied heavily on friends and family to do their work, and avoided work by manipulating their teachers. While helping them succeed and avoid social devaluation, these strategies reduced the intensity of their education, put them behind other college-bound students, and created dependencies and habits that were difficult to replicate in more challenging, geographically distant, college settings. Thus, in their attempt to adapt successfully to one setting, they unwittingly learned to be learning disabled for a subsequent setting.

Another example frequently cited was the transition from school to work. In educational settings, people enjoyed a whole complex of professional and accommodative procedures that had been established for their benefit. Although these procedures were sometimes resisted by parents, professionals, and students, they represented prescribed roles and enforceable regulations that all parties were expected to follow. In the work world, however, no comparable structures existed. In fact, few employers knew anything about learning disabilities or the accommodations and adaptive equipment that might be needed by a person with learning problems. Thus, work environments were often perceived as more ambiguous and unpredictable than educational settings, even though adaptations were usually inexpensive and relatively easy to arrange. However, because of such setting-specific differences, individuals were virtually assured of experiencing adaptive problems when moving from school to work situations.

Although most college students developed their own informal adaptations, many of which were setting-centered, they still used such formal accommodations as extra time and student tutors, which were not often duplicated in work situations. Such reliance by students was perfectly appropriate as long as it was not assumed to be applicable to their next setting. Often people needed to develop new strategies for what they anticipated as their next environment—usually work. However, they were seldom provided helpful transitional experiences in which they could develop these strategies within real work situations and under actual working conditions in their field of study.

Institutional incentives. It was also clear from people's descriptions that learning disabilities were not just unwittingly "learned" because of misguided intervention methods. They were also *created* by educational organizations. Schools and colleges employed diagnosticians, special education teachers and tutors, and other specialized personnel to identify, advise, support, and instruct people with diagnosed learning disabilities. Many colleges had incentives to provide labels for low-achieving students who sought admission, or who had been admitted but were not performing well academically. Public two-year colleges frequently served lower-achieving students who might be college material, but presently could not gain admission to a four-year school. As one college learning specialist related, it was easier to assist students successfully with a combination of tools such as academic accommodations and tutoring than with tutoring alone. However, formal accommodations could only be provided if an individual had been diagnosed as learning disabled. Also, because the effectiveness of specialized personnel was at least partially tied to their success at serving low-achieving students, and because they often provided the testing required to formally label someone, such personnel had considerable incentives and latitude to label the individuals they were serving.

Some private two-year and four-year colleges, although not mandated to serve students with academic problems, depended financially upon the admission and success of students with learning disabilities. Thus, special offices were established to encourage low-achieving high school students to apply to their school. Such offices were also designed to seek out students who might need their assistance. Students with mediocre high school records reportedly enrolled at a private four-year school and were contacted by a member of the school's specialized staff. In some cases students were advised to be tested and to enroll in a study group for students with learning disabilities. When one student asked how the staff member had singled her out, she was told that all students were screened for "potential" learning disabilities. It seemed clear that such specialized offices were oriented not only to help students who arrived with a label, but to label students who arrived needing help.

Functions of Labeling

Whereas the conditions surrounding labeling were inconsistent and complex, formal classifications had the consistent and important effect of redefining who people were, and what was wrong with them. It redefined them from being poor students to being learning disabled, and through the professionals, services, and placements that followed, they were socialized into a new social role: handicapped person.

Individual responses to this new identity were mixed. In the presence of specific expectations, many subscribed to the definition of their inadequate academic performance as a neurogenic symptom of dysfunction. Although the LD label did not alleviate all of the confusion they felt about their situation, or lead to a remedial cure, it (a) provided a central, organizing focus to their problems; (b) brought a semblance of order to their disordered experiences; (c) represented a more valued interpretation of their problems; and (d) led to important accommodative service benefits not available to them as unlabeled persons.

The designation also had negative effects. It (a) reinforced the belief that incompetence emanated from their personal deficiencies, (b) raised anxieties about genetic dysfunction, (c) fostered a generalized notion of personal incompetence, (d) obscured the environmental determinants of their learning problems, (e) minimized setting-change solutions to their problems, and (f) led to stigmatizing professional treatments. Thus, the learning disabilities classification, and its neurogenic/individual emphasis created as many problems as it solved.

It is surprising how little evidence exists to link physiogenic deficits and learning disabilities (Coles, 1987; Kavale & Forness, 1985; McGuinness, 1986). Apparently, however, the medical metaphor, with its person-centered emphasis, serves useful societal as well as individual functions. Senf (1987), for example, has termed learning disabilities a "sociological sponge" that wipes up the messes left by regular education and cleanses its ills (p. 87). In this way, the metaphor serves to absolve our entire culture, and its culture-bearing agents and institutions, of responsibility both for people's learning problems and for systemic solutions to those problems. Within prevailing social policy and practice the emphasis is on making students "better," while minimizing or ignoring the extra-individual forces that—as has been illustrated in this study—often create, perpetuate, and exacerbate people's learning "problems." Thus, the medical metaphor may be considered a societal management strategy for avoiding a far broader issue: school failure. The broader problem is managed and obscured by our narrow and continuing explanatory preoccupation with individual dysfunction.

As Caplan and Nelson (1973, p. 202) have pointed out, a neurogenic explanation for school failure fits nicely into our prevailing societal interpretations of "social problems" in general, where a person-blame causal attribution bias dominates our research and practice activities, and where practitioners assume that "if the shoe doesn't fit, something is wrong with your foot." These authors have argued further that every society attempts to characterize its deviant members as a source of problems. Through its existing institutions, it socializes its citizens (including social scientists and practitioners) to accept as a state of mind "a world disastrously out of tune with human needs."

Changing the Model

From this investigation it seems evident that people's learning problems are related to a far broader and more complex array of extra-individual forces than is implied by the prevailing societal definitions of learning disabilities (see also Linney & Seidman, 1989). I recommend that the prevailing conceptualization of learning disabilities be replaced by a less medicalized, more community-based orientation in which people experiencing academic difficulties would be able to obtain intensive remedial and accommodative services without the formal designation of dysfunction and consequent segregation.

This is not a new proposal. Numerous educational researchers have called for abandoning the medical model with its limited utility, and adopting conceptualizations of learning problems "that replace disease with difference, chronicity with transiency, and pessimism with optimism" (Brown & Campione, 1986; Kavale & Forness, 1985, p. 62; McGuinness, 1986). Reynolds, Wang, and Walberg (1987) and Stainback and Stainback (1984) have suggested that the problems of classification, overidentification, and poor treatment outcomes require the elimination of the learning disability category altogether, a suspension of existing eligibility rules and regulations, and a change to a noncategorical system of services (Chalfant, 1989). These recommendations clearly signal a move away from strictly person-focused special services to a more system-change, integrated model of assistance. As Biklen and Zollers (1986) have rightfully concluded, "the interests of learning disabled students are those of all students, and the solutions for students with learning disabilities are inextricably linked to the future of education in general" (p. 585).

Although Chalfant (1989), Gallagher (1987), and others consider such recommendations "extreme, imprudent, and unnecessary" (Chalfant, 1989, p. 394), and fraught with difficulties, they have suggested some reforms that appear to reinforce the call for policy changes. Chalfant, for example, termed the Regular Education Initiative (which recommends that all students be taught in regular classrooms adapted to meet their needs, rather than be removed for all or part of the day to a resource room for individualized/small group instruction) a "promising alternative to special education services" (p. 394). In addition, Chalfant has argued for the waiver of regulations that prohibit nondisabled students from receiving needed assistance, suggested that more comprehensive and intensive alternatives to the resource room model need to be found, and called for heightened collaboration between special and regular educators in both schools and colleges to help meet the integration objectives of the Regular Education Initiative.

Academic Alternatives

Efforts should be made to implement the broad mandates of inclusive education by focusing on school reforms that will enable students to receive as intensive help as necessary without formal labeling or segregated services. In order to accomplish this, concerted system-wide efforts could be undertaken to promote a sense of educational pluralism by which "having a problem" is considered an expected and typical part of school structures and culture. An atmosphere should be created in which students can get the assistance they need to master their present and subsequent environments, and do so within an atmosphere of tolerance, valuation, and equality.

Biklen and Zollers (1986) have reviewed the literature and identified some educational practices that they believe offer valuable alternatives to a pull-out, medical/pathogenic model of services. These practices provide examples of instructional intensity and adaptation without the stigmatizing effects of segregation. It is beyond the scope of this chapter to describe each of these alternatives in detail. However, the list includes the following alternatives: (a) prereferral school teams (see Chalfant, Van Dusen Psyh, & Moultrie, 1979); (b) cooperative learning programs (see Slavin, Madden, & Leavey, 1984; Johnson & Johnson, 1986); (c) consulting teacher (see Knight, Meyers, Whitcomb,

Hasazi, & Nevin, 1981); (d) alternative learning/renewed classrooms (see Wang & Walberg, 1985); and (e) effective schools research (see Biklen, 1985; Bloom, 1976).

Naturally, students with learning disabilities were under initial pressures to follow the diagnostic and prescriptive paths laid out by parents and by teachers and other professionals. However, those who wished to improve their academic performance and thereby avoid the segregating and stigmatizing aspects of existing treatment programs had to assume a very active role in defining and managing their problems on their own terms. Many times this meant supplementing and even contradicting established, recommended interventions, and deploying unique and creative setting-change strategies. Such strategies are little acknowledged in the literature, but represent an essential part of people's responses to their situations. Thus, in addition to a heightened emphasis on intensive, integrated remedial services, there should also be a sharper focus on the development of directed and supervised coping strategies that focus on changing educational and employment settings and on circumventing individual deficiencies. After studying coping strategies of college students, Cowen (1988, p. 164) recommended that "intervention strategies for persons of all ages with learning disabilities should focus on coping strategies for compensating or bypassing skill deficits as well as the remediation of skill deficits." Thus, as young adults progress from elementary to high school to postsecondary activities, they need assistance in finding ways around their problems and in securing the assistance and support of people around them. In real (not simulated) integrated school, college, and/or work situations, students should be helped to develop specific, individualized covert and overt compensatory and remedial procedures that address both their learning difficulties and their social preferences for certain kinds of assistance.

Given the importance of developing relevant, compensatory skills, it is likely that students who can function without special class placements in primary and secondary school; conceal their disability; and learn specific, individualized (formal and informal) coping methods within these settings will be better prepared for the world they will eventually enter. Such individuals will have more closely experienced the conditions that will exist in their "next" environments. At all educational levels and at home, persons should be provided more than remedial assistance. They should be helped to develop and apply setting-change strategies for circumventing their skill deficits within the real community situations they will eventually enter.

This is not to argue for the elimination of public disclosure of one's disability, remedial skill acquisition, or formal accommodations. In fact, there exists a critical need for more widespread education of the business community to the employment potential of people with disabilities, for the improvement of remedial methods, and for the provision of more widely available accommodations, especially in high school and school-to-work activities. Also needed are modifications of existing accommodations, such as textbooks on tape, in order to make them more useable to people with learning difficulties. Expansion and modification of such adaptive options would help to ensure that services are based on individualized priorities and preferences, not diagnosis; that segregated settings are abolished; that students are exposed early and often, and with as much on-site, naturally occurring support as needed, to the real world settings and expectations to which they aspire.

Employment Alternatives

For some people, employment represented a welcome challenge, and a change from the constraining arenas of education and family. For others who had grown accustomed to the structured, familiar world of education, work could be mysterious and formidable. Presumably because of the difficult transition from school to work, nearly everyone experienced problems, discouragements, and self-doubts about whether they could achieve successful employment. However, in most cases employment problems could be as easily attributable to restrictive training and educational experiences and unhelpful employment practices as to individual deficits. Specifically, employment difficulties appeared to occur because most individuals (a) had very narrow work knowledge and experiences, especially in employment areas of interest to them; (b) perceived their problems as intra-individual rather than environmental; and (c) received little or no assistance in adapting to desired employment situations.

Improving real work experiences and support groups. People's lack of work experience was a primary obstacle to developing effective management strategies that depended on knowledge of setting-specific factors. Those entering the work force were entering a world in which they had minimal standing or experience and which, in turn, had little experience or familiarity with them. Once they had left the educational environment, the "LD student" designation faded, along with its concomitant and predictable services, accommodations, and professionals. In the employment arena there were no institutionally prescribed roles or activities assigned to persons with learning disabilities, no support groups, no structured procedures to tell supervisors or bosses about their disability, and no special tutoring arrangements or time extensions. Everything was negotiable, and because most individuals knew little about specific work requirements or how to meet them, they did not know what to negotiate. Thus, they usually asked for nothing, even though they may have needed some accommodations.

For many individuals, the work place was the first setting in which they could enter and function with no formal, prescribed identity or role. They were required to carve out their own identity and relationships, depending upon how they defined themselves, presented themselves to others, and managed the tasks and situations they encountered. For many this process proved troublesome, but if mastered was extremely liberating.

White (1985) has argued that the schools have neither adequately prepared LD young adults for the social/affective facets of adult life, nor taught them what to expect when they leave school. As noted earlier in this chapter, schools and colleges must change dramatically how they prepare students to enter the world of work. They should expose individuals to real community work settings, assist them in approaching and defining themselves to employers, and acquaint them with formal and informal, covert and noncovert ways of changing the work setting and obtaining support from those around them, such as co-workers and/or supervisors. This sort of instruction is not entirely new to most schools or colleges. It has been conducted through community internships, summer programs, transitional programs of all kinds, and job support groups. The latter have been recommended by Michaels (1989) for employees with learning disabilities who do not want to reveal their label to supervisors and/or co-workers. Such groups have met during evening hours and have included professional and/or self-help emphases. Individuals in the study who used support gatherings in college often found them helpful, especially the self-help component. However, they suggested that such groups include nondisabled students to avoid some of the social stigma connected with "special" services. To avoid this problem, persons with learning disabilities should be assisted to find and join job seeking/retention and/or employment support groups conducted for the general public or student population, and operated by local employment services and college or community counseling centers.

Legitimizing effective coping strategies. Many individuals in the current study manipulated their work environment and the people in it, devising innovative and productive strategies for doing their job. Most often such strategies were done surreptitiously, learned through direct experiences in real work situations, and viewed as critical to people's employment successes. Such strategies constituted important determinants of employment success.

Interestingly, the setting-change orientation so critical to implementing these strategies has been notably absent from the learning disabilities literature, especially as applied to employment situations. A notable exception has been the recent movement toward a natural supports approach to supported employment (see Nisbet & Hagner, 1988; Hagner, Murphy, & Rogan, in press). Supported employment professionals have increasingly emphasized the use of naturally occurring (as opposed to professionally imposed) sources of worksite support, and the pursuit of setting-change adaptive strategies in order to help people succeed in employment situations. Although supported employment has focused primarily on people with the most severe disabilities, and has had little impact on LD services, I believe this literature has important implications for the LD field. I will describe these contributions later in this chapter.

The socializing thrust of most professional efforts has been toward teaching people to accept their disability as a fixed intra-individual reality (Murphy, Scheer, Murphy, & Mack, 1988), and to integrate this narrow perspective into their vocational lives. According to Murphy et al. (1988), such a narrow perspective, although prevalent within the disability field, is particularly unhelpful because it socializes people to passively accept the prescribed definitions, stereotypic identities, and overgeneralized roles too often foisted on them by well-intentioned professionals. Examples of such definitions, identities, and roles are plentiful within the vocational rehabilitation literature, but are contradicted by some findings of the current study.

Writing about the vocational rehabilitation of persons with learning disabilities, Hershenson (1984), Rosenthal (1989), and Simpson and Umbach (1989) described the behavioral characteristics and tendencies of adults with learning disabilities. The authors noted that people with LD suffered from, among other things, low self-esteem; poor reality testing; unrealistic expectations; exploratory learning passivity; learned helplessness; an inability to accurately assess their strengths, weaknesses, interests, and values; impaired decision making "of all kinds" (Rosenthal, 1989, pp. 56 & 63); emotional instability; social imperception; "more affective deficits than strengths" (Simpson & Umbach, 1989, p. 53); frustration; depression; and lack of emotional and temper control.

From this list of behavioral attributes arose suggestions for effective vocational counseling. Hershenson (1984) suggested professionals work to help people with learning disabilities understand their disability and improve their self-image, for "only after the client has come to accept the nature of the specific disability, and established a realistic self-image, can exploration of vocational concerns be productively undertaken" (p. 43). Simpson and Umbach (1989) recommended that (a) people who perseverate or dislike change be placed in repetitious jobs; (b) jobs be avoided that require constant adaptation to changing circumstances, or impatient employers; and (c) quiet workplaces be found for persons with auditory perceptual problems.

Like most of the professional literature, these descriptions cast learning disabilities as fixed or real attributes residing within persons. However, one of the preeminent findings of the current study was that learning disabled behaviors were ecologically fluid entities, which could emanate from a variety of extra-individual sources, and which required remediation of settings as much as self.

Despite Hershenson's (1984) suggestions, interviewees in the current study illustrated that knowledge of self and disability were fluid dynamics that changed with changing experiences and situations. In fact, people reported that they had learned the most about themselves and their disability after becoming immersed in specific educational, vocational, and social settings, and by learning (and sometimes failing) to manipulate the people and requirements they encountered. Thus, rather than advocating that counseling and teaching about self and disability will reveal fixed realities that should form the basis for meaningful vocational actions, professionals should consider the reverse: that meaningful vocational actions lead to realistic knowledge of self and disability, and that such knowledge changes as one's actions expand.

Simpson and Umbach (1989) also offered vocational counseling suggestions for adults with LD, presenting a format for matching people and job settings. However, in addition to minimizing the vocational decision making of those being served, their recommendations promote the perspective that people who do not fit easily into existing job situations should change their expectations, definitions, interests, and roles, and find another setting into which they can more easily fit. Unfortunately, these proposals also contain several elements that were contraindicated by interviewees in the present study.

Within the current study were numerous examples of people who functioned well in jobs because they did *not* give up their expectations and interests, and developed effective ways to circumvent their problems by manipulating requirements, expectations, and/or people in order to succeed.

It should not be concluded that of those interviewed, none had any of the behavioral characteristics cited by the aforementioned writers. Some did, although many did not. Moreover, there are many *non-LD persons* who also manifest such tendencies. More importantly, the present study should raise the question as to whether these attributes merely represent the stereotyped identities and overgeneralized roles Murphy et al. (1988) warned about. In fact, many interviewees were found to possess behavioral tendencies that contrasted sharply with those listed. For example, many individuals demonstrated obvious social perception; great control of their emotions, temper, and frustrations; high esteem and expectations for themselves; and extensive exploratory school and work activities. Why have such characteristics and behavioral tendencies not been mentioned in the field's literature? They were certainly displayed prominently as interviewees defined themselves and described their lives. Some interviewees pointed specifically to these activities and attributes as important ingredients for their successes in certain situations and settings.

Another important ingredient in people's vocational successes was their ability to obtain assistance from others and to adapt a job to their strengths. Such a focus has much in common with the natural support approach to supported employment mentioned earlier in this chapter. Although designed primarily for those with severe disabilities, this approach is relevant for people of varied characteristics, including those diagnosed as LD.

In applying natural support strategies to vocational situations, practitioners address setting-specific and setting-change elements of work sites. For example, they look for jobs which include: a) friendly, supportive co-workers, b) flexible work routines and job sharing arrangements, c) physical proximity to others, d) intersecting or overlapping tasks, e) co-workers of the same gender and similar age, f) a stable work force, and g) an open versus compartmentalized physical layout (Hagner, Murphy, & Rogan, in press). Once on-site, natural support practitioners attempt to gain the assistance of co-workers and supervisors in carrying out those tasks with which a disabled person might have difficulty, and in becoming a friend and source of social support to the new employee (Racino, in press). Professionals may also assist employees with disabilities—and those around them—to change work arrangements, routines, and requirements in order to maximize their strengths.

In many ways, natural support methods represent formalized versions of the strategies people in the present study applied to the educational and vocational situations they encountered. While people labeled LD may not need the same level of professional and co-worker assistance as those with more severe disabilities, they could benefit greatly from learning and applying these strategies in school, college, and work. On the professional side, combining knowledge of a natural support approach with the coping strategies described by individuals in this book would provide a strong foundation upon which to build a network of natural support and coping services.

In general, the vocational rehabilitation field has failed many of those it has been charged with assisting. By adopting a primarily deficit-laden, person-change mentality, rehabilitation professionals have inadequately acknowledged that people's problems emanate from more than intrapsychic dysfunction, and that to succeed, individuals need to understand and address the setting-specific obstacles (including those imposed by professional beliefs and services) that impede their successful functioning within the community. These inadequacies were underscored by interviewee descriptions of their often successful efforts to manipulate and change, rather than to abandon, desired vocational settings.

Educating employers. Many employment problems reported by persons in the study appeared to result as much from narrow hiring and training practices by the employer as from individual deficits. Most employers were preoccupied with finding the "just right" employee to fill a prescribed job, and were unprepared to deal effectively with persons who learned differently by selecting alternative tasks and/or rearranging the job for them in order to maximize their specific skills.

Certainly educational and vocational rehabilitation organizations bear major responsibilities for preparing students for the vocational world. However, enough is known about how employers can discriminate against applicants who do not fit readily into their "job-ready" categories to recognize that the burden of change must be shifted from the individual job applicant to the employer. Progress toward implementing such a shift nationally was recently made with the passage of the Americans With Disabilities Act of 1990 (ADA). This legislation extends the antidiscrimination provisions of the Rehabilitation Act of 1973 to include not just federal contractors and federally funded employers, but all employers. Moreover, under the ADA the burden of proof in the hiring area switches from the job applicant to the employer. In cases of alleged discrimination, the employer has to demonstrate the fairness and validity of his or her hiring, training, and promotion practices. This shift should serve as an important incentive for employers to provide, create, and support the kind of accommodations and compensatory strategies that persons in this study had to develop and apply surreptitiously.

It will not suffice, however, to pressure employers merely to drop their discriminatory practices. Before they adopt a truly progressive attitude toward hiring, training, and promoting persons with disabilities, employers must be instructed on how to think differently about their jobs and work environment. Specifically, employers should be shown *how to*: (a) develop fair and flexible hiring criteria; (b) implement systematic, individualized training procedures; (c) restructure jobs to accommodate individuals with specific skills and problems; (d) use adaptive technology; and (e) apply creative ways of supporting their employees through the sharing of job tasks and/or working cooperatively. Through such assistance professionals could help more employers discover, as many already have, that flexible workplace arrangements often lead to higher production and job satisfaction, and to lower attrition for all employees, not just those with disabilities.

Over the years, many public relations campaigns have been aimed at employers to promote hiring of persons with disabilities. Recently, such initiatives have been proposed to improve the employment circumstances of persons labeled learning disabled (see Minskoff, Sautter, Hoffmann, & Hawkes, 1987). Such campaigns, however well intentioned, are likely misguided because they inadvertently may reinforce stereotyping, perpetuate the idea of learning disabilities as a homogeneous condition, and tacitly encourage employers to follow prescribed responses when dealing with labeled applicants/ employees.

Focusing on the purported "benefits" of hiring and/or promoting specific, labeled people may perpetuate negative stereotyping even if the focus is intended as positive. Emphasizing the label, however positively, detracts from the idiosyncratic characteristics of individuals. Moreover, awareness of an employee's label does not provide employers with the kind of concrete assistance they need to train individuals to do specific jobs and to provide the kind of flexible, modifiable work setting that will accommodate employees with diverse characteristics and skills.

Persons in the study expressed a preference for disclosing themselves in their own way and at their own time. Depending upon how they assessed the employment situation, they developed specific strategies for informing supervisors or co-workers about their label. Because public relations campaigns may lead to early identification of job applicants as "learning disabled," such initiatives might undermine individual disclosure preferences and reduce the latitude successful employees reportedly required to maneuver within their specific worksites.

Social Alternatives

Within the field's literature it is presumed that many persons with learning disabilities have social/interpersonal difficulties attributable to their disability. These deficiencies are considered serious problems that negatively affect the quality of people's lives, magnify their learning problems, reduce their social and vocational options, and require specialized, intensive social skills remediation (Cartledge, 1989; Gresham, 1988; Hallahan et al., 1985; Kavale, 1988; Lerner, 1985). However, the accounts of people interviewed for the present study painted a different picture of their social competencies and the kind of services that might be helpful.

For the most part, those interviewed described typical and satisfying social lives, despite the humiliation of segregated classes and the oft-mentioned dependence on others for help. In fact, schools appeared to create more social distance between labeled students and their nonlabeled peers than did the purported disability. Segregated classes separated people from their friends and highlighted their academic differences. The label also created confusion among students. Because learning disabilities were almost never intrusive or obvious in everyday interactions, people were considered socially normal by their friends outside of school. But many interviewees remembered feeling socially isolated following their enrollment in special classes attended by students with highly stigmatizing labels. Such placements were described as far more disruptive to people's social lives than their academic problems.

Contrary to much of the learning disabilities literature on social skills, most of the interviewees actively pursued social contacts and demonstrated considerable social sophistication, guile, and success. The social predicament people found themselves in due to special classes and the need for academic assistance from others stimulated many to pursue extracurricular and extraschool activities, and to cultivate social contacts outside the classroom. It was particularly important for some individuals, devalued intellectually, to avoid more generalized social devaluation. To combat this possibility people employed a variety of strategies, such as "finding a strong suit," which consisted of pursuing activities in which they could excel. These activities ranged from sports to art to car repair. Thus, rather than isolating themselves socially and risking widespread social rejection, many people worked hard at proving themselves to their friends.

Because people frequently depended on the help of others in academic and vocational settings, they reported using a wide variety of well-honed social skills in order to function effectively in those settings. Well-executed, manipulative social competencies effectively camouflaged or compensated for performance problems, reduced the negative effects of the label, and gained the confidence and acceptance of others.

In some instances people's social needs could become intimately entangled with their need for assistance. Some students sought out peers because they could type, took good class notes, belonged to a study group, or were in a position to alleviate job pressures. People who provided help became good friends, sometimes spouses. And good friends and spouses sometimes became invaluable sources of help.

In some cases people's social isolation was self-imposed. To succeed academically people reportedly had to spend significant amounts of time studying. Such time-consuming activities often interfered with their social lives, especially in college. As one student remarked: "I spend so much time reading or studying, I don't have time for anything else." Thus, many interviewees believed that some amount of social withdrawal was necessary and self-imposed, and did not reflect social rejection by others.

It should not be concluded that no one in the study experienced interpersonal and/or psychological problems, or that such difficulties were not serious. People did complain of social stigma and social isolation. However, these problems could be ascribed to far more numerous factors and circumstances than intra-individual dysfunction.

In light of the idiosyncratic, complex, and sophisticated nature of people's social interactions, and of the social problems people attributed to professional interventions, professionals should reconsider their proposed solutions to people's "social deficits." This is especially urgent for those who have called for specialized social remediation programs that rely on professional labels and prescriptions, and separate placements. Certainly some individuals could benefit from formal social skills competency programs. However, there is no evidence that persons with learning disabilities, as a group, must learn these skills differently than do other persons.

SOME CONCLUDING COMMENTS ABOUT "REAL" LEARNING DISABILITIES

Implicit in the comments of people in this book is the message that their learning difficulties may have been created, perpetuated, and exaggerated as much by the interactive responses of others to their "not measuring up" or "fitting in" as by any organic dysfunction. This raises the question as to whether those in the sample were "truly" learning disabled.

Of course, the questions of what is a "real" learning disability, and how is it properly determined, are among the most controversial issues in the field (Chalfant, 1989; Hammill, 1990; Keogh, 1988). On the conceptual side, Hammill (1990, p. 74) has contended that the situation has improved, concluding that the field's "professionally viable" (p. 82) definitions have been reduced from eleven to four, around which there is a 74% level of professional agreement. By Hammill's own account, however, there still exists a 25% level of disagreement among eight competing definitions (p. 82).

On the applied side, Chalfant (1989, p. 393) has argued that:

The greatest divergence of opinion within the field of learning disabilities relates to diagnosis. There is no consensus concerning the diagnostic procedures that should be used to specify the nature of a student's problems or the criteria for classifying a student as learning disabled.

Despite claims of an emerging professional consensus, there still seems to be considerable conceptual and practical dissonance regarding the definition of learning disabilities. Further, it is felt that people included in the present study were labeled under conceptual and clinical circumstances similar to those that exist for most persons undergoing diagnostic testing. Thus, questions about the accuracy and reality of this group's diagnosis could likely be raised around the selection of virtually any sample of people.

In fact, the purpose of this book is not to solve the definitional problems plaguing the learning disabilities field. The purpose is to document the experiences of those who have been labeled, presuming that the perceived consequences of their diagnosis, including subsequent reactions and treatments, would provide valuable information about the label, the sources and process of labeling, the people who have assigned the label, and those to whom the label has been assigned.

The reality is that learning disability is not just a problem for those who possess real neurogenic dysfunctions, but for all those who must contend with the social consequences of the label. Dexter (1961) has reminded us that such consequences are for the people so designated the "realest of realities." These consequences will exist as long as the learning disabled label is conferred, whether or not professionals ever can claim, as McGrady (1987, p. 108) has exhorted, to separate the "truly learning disabled from the impostors."

References

Adelman, H. S., & Taylor, L. (1983). *Learning disabilities in perspective.* Glenville, IL: Scott, Foresman.

Algozzine, B. (1985). Low achiever differentiation: Where's the beef? *Exceptional Children, 52,* 72–75.

Algozzine, B., & Ysseldyke, J. E. (1983). Learning disabilities as a subset of school failure: The oversophistication of a concept. *Exceptional Children, 50,* 242–246.

American Psychiatric Association. (1980). *Diagnostic and statistical manual of mental disorders* (3rd ed.). Washington, DC: Author.

Balint, M. (1972). *The doctor, his patient, and the illness.* New York: International Universities Press.

Becker, H. S. (1966). *Outsiders: Studies in the sociology of deviance.* New York: Free Press.

Becker, H. S. (1973). Labelling theory reconsidered. In H. S. Becker. *Outsiders: Studies in the sociology of deviance* (2nd ed.). New York: Free Press.

Berman, A. (1981). Research associating learning disabilities with juvenile delinquency. In J. Gottlieb & S. Strichart (Eds.), *Developmental theory and research in learning disabilities* (pp. 341–367). Baltimore, MD: University Park Press.

Berman, A., & Seigal, A. W. (1976). Adaptive and learning skills in juvenile delinquents: A neuropsychological analysis. *Journal of Learning Disabilities, 9,* 583–590.

Biklen, D. (1985). *Achieving the complete school: Strategies for effective mainstreaming.* New York: Teachers College Press.

Biklen, D., & Zollers, N. (1986). The focus of advocacy in the LD field. *Journal of Learning Disabilities, 19,* 579–586.

Biller, E. F., & White, W. J. (1989). Comparing special education and vocational rehabilitation in serving persons with specific learning disabilities. *Rehabilitation Counseling Bulletin, 33,* 4–17.

Bloom, B. (1976). *Human characteristics of school learning.* New York: McGraw-Hill.

Brown, A. L., & Campione, J. C. (1986). Psychological theory and the study of learning disabilities. *American Psychologist, 41,* 1059–1068.

Brown, D. (1985). *Steps to independence for people with learning disabilities.* Washington, DC: Goodwill Industries of America.

Buchanan, M., & Wolf, J. S. (1986). A comprehensive study of learning disabled adults. *Journal of Learning Disabilities, 19,* 34–38.

Caplan, N., & Nelson, S. D. (1973). On being useful: The nature and consequences of psychological research on social problems. *American Psychologist, 28,* 199–211.

Cartledge, C. (1989). Social skills and vocational success for workers with learning disabilities. *Rehabilitation Counseling Bulletin, 33,* 74–79.

Chalfant, J. C. (1987). Providing services to all students with learning problems: Implications for policy and programs. In S. Vaughn & C. S. Bos (Eds.), *Research in learning disabilities: Issues and future directions* (pp. 239–251). Boston: Little, Brown.

Chalfant, J. C. (1989). Learning disabilities: Policy issues and promising approaches. *American Psychologist, 44,* 392–398.

Chalfant, J. C., Van Dusen Psyh, M., & Moultrie, R. (1979). Teacher assistance teams: A model for within-building problem solving. *Learning Disabilities Quarterly, 2,* 85–96.

Clinard, M. B., & Meier, R. F. (1985). *Sociology of deviant behavior.* New York: Holt, Rinehart, & Winston.

Coles, G. S. (1987). *The learning mystique: A critical look at learning disabilities.* New York: Pantheon.

Comptroller General of the U.S. (1977). *Learning disabilities: The link to delinquency should be determined, but schools should do more.* Washington, DC: General Accounting Office.

Cowen, S. E. (1988). Coping strategies of university students with learning disabilities. *Journal of Learning Disabilities, 21,* 161–164.

Cruickshank, W., Morse, W., & Johns, J. (1980). *Learning disabilities: The struggle from adolescence to adulthood.* Syracuse, NY: Syracuse University Press.

Dembo, T. (1970). The utilization of psychological knowledge in rehabilitation. *Welfare in Review, 8,* 1–7.

Deschler, D., Alley, G., Warner, M., & Schumaker, J. (1984). Instructional practices for promoting skill acquisition and generalization in severely learning disabled adolescents. *Learning Disabilities Quarterly, 4* (4), 415–421.

Deschler, D. D., Schumaker, J. B., & Lenz, B. K. (1984). Academic and cognitive interventions for L.D. adolescents. *Journal of Learning Disabilities, 17,* 108–117.

Dexter, L. (1961). On the politics and sociology and stupidity in our society. *Social Problems, 9,* 221–228.

Divorky, D. (1974). Education's last victim: The LD kid. *Learning,* 20–26.

Eighth annual report to Congress on the implementation of P.L. 94-142: The Education of All Handicapped Children Act. (1986). Washington, DC: U.S. Dept. of Education, Office of Special Education.

Falfard, M., & Haubrick, P. A. (1981). Vocational and social adjustment of learning disabled young adults: A follow-up study. *Learning Disabilities Quarterly, 4,* 122–130.

Foster, G., Yesseldyke, J., & Reese, J. I. (1975). I never would have seen it if I hadn't believed it. *Exceptional Children, 41,* 469–473.

Friedson, E. (1965). Disability as social deviance. In R. Sussman (Ed.), *Sociology and rehabilitation.* Washington, DC: American Sociology Association.

Gallagher, J. J. (1987). Public policy and the malleability of children. In J. Gallagher & C. Ramey (Eds.), *The malleability of children* (pp. 199–208). Baltimore, MD: Paul H. Brookes.

Garfinkel, H., & Sacks, H. (1970). The formal properties of practical actions. In J. C. McKinney & E. Tiryakiian (Eds.), *Theoretical sociology* (pp. 337–366). New York: Appleton-Century-Crofts.

Glaser, B. G. (1978). *Theoretical sensitivity.* Mill Valley, CA: Sociology Press.

Glaser, B. G., & Strauss, A. L. (1967). *The discovery of grounded theory: Strategies for qualitative research.* Hawthorne, NY: Aldine.

Gould, S. J. (1982). *The mismeasure of man.* New York: W. W. Norton.

Gresham, F. M. (1988). Social competence and motivational characteristics of learning disabled students. In M. C. Wang, M. C. Reynolds, & H. J. Walberg (Eds.), *Handbook of special education: Research and practice* (Vol. 2, pp. 283–302). New York: Pergamon Press.

Growick, B., & Dowdy, C. (1989). Interchange: Preface. *Rehabilitation Counseling Bulletin, 33,* 2–3.

Hagner, D., Murphy, S., & Rogan, P. (in press). Facilitating natural supports in the workplace. *Journal of Rehabilitation.*

Hallahan, D. P., Kauffman, J. M., & Lloyd, J. W. (1985). *Introduction to learning disabilities.* Englewood Cliffs, NJ: Prentice-Hall.

Hammill, D. D. (1990). On defining learning disabilities: An emerging consensus. *Journal of Learning Disabilities, 23,* 74–84.

Hershenson, D. B. (1984). Vocational counseling with learning disabled adults. *Journal of Rehabilitation, 50,* 40–44.

Hewitt, J. P. (1984). *Self and society. A symbolic interactionist social psychology.* Boston: Allyn & Bacon.

Hiebert, B., Wong, B., & Hubter, M. (1982). Affective influences in learning disabled adolescents. *Learning Disabilities Quarterly, 5,* 334–343.

Hoffman, F. J., Sheldon, K. L., Minskoff, E. H., Sautter, S. W., Steidle, E. F., Baker, D. P., Bailey, B., & Echols, L. D. (1987). Needs of learning disabled adults. *Journal of Learning Disabilities, 20,* 43–52.

Johnson, D., & Johnson, R. (1986). Mainstreaming and cooperative learning strategies. *Exceptional Children, 52,* 553–561.

Johnston, C. (1984). The learning disabled adolescent and young adult: An overview and critique of current practices. *Journal of Learning Disabilities, 17,* 386–391.

Kavale, K. (1988). The long term consequences of learning disabilities. In M. C. Wang, M. C. Reynolds, & H. J. Walberg (Eds.), *Handbook of special education: Research and practice* (Vol. 2, pp. 303–344). New York: Pergamon Press.

Kavale, K., & Forness, S. (1985). *The science of learning disabilities.* San Diego, CA: College-Hill Press.

Keogh, B. K. (1987). A shared attribute model of learning disabilities. In S. Vaughn & C. S. Bos (Eds.), *Research in learning disabilities: Issues and future directions* (pp. 3–18). Boston: Little, Brown.

Keogh, B. K. (1988). Learning disability: Diversity in search of order. In M. C. Wang, M. C. Reynolds, & H. J. Walberg (Eds.), *Handbook of special education: Research and practice* (Vol. 2, pp. 225–252). New York: Pergamon Press.

Kirk, S. A. (1987). Intervention research in learning disabilities. In S. Vaughn & C. S. Bos (Eds.), *Research in learning disabilities: Issues and future directions* (pp. 173–184). Boston: Little, Brown.

Knight, M., Meyers, H., Whitcomb, P., Hasazi, S., & Nevin, A. (1981). A four year evaluation of consulting teacher service. *Council for Children with Behavioral Disorders, 6,* 92–100.

Kolligan, J., & Sternberg, R. J. (1987). Intelligence, information processing, and specific learning disabilities. *Journal of Learning Disabilities, 20,* 8–16.

Lambert, N. (1986). Learning disabilities: The whole truth. *Contemporary Psychology, 31,* 840–841.

Lane, M. (1977). A reconsideration of context: Perspectives on prediction—Mote in the eye. *American Psychologist, 32,* 1056–1059.

Lane, B. A. (1980). The relationship of learning disabilities to juvenile delinquency: Current status. *Journal of Learning Disabilities, 13,* 425–434.

Lerner, J. W. (1981). *Learning disabilities: Theories, diagnosis, and teaching strategies* (3rd ed.). Boston: Houghton Mifflin.

Lerner, J. W. (1985). *Learning disabilities.* Boston: Houghton Mifflin.

Levitin, T. E. (1975). Deviants as active participants in the labeling process: The visually handicapped. *Social Problems, 22,* 548–557.

Linney, J. A., & Seidman, E. (1989). The future of schooling. *American Psychologist, 44,* 336–342.

Lloyd, J. W. (1988). Direct academic intervention in learning disabilities. In M. C. Wang, M. C. Reynolds, & H. J. Walberg (Eds.), *Handbook of special education: Research and practice* (Vol. 2, pp. 345–366). New York: Pergamon Press.

Lofland, J. (1971). *Analyzing social settings.* Belmont, CA: Wadsworth.

Madden, N., & Slavin, R. (1983). Mainstreaming students with mild handicaps. *Review of Educational Research, 53,* 519–569.

Mars, L. (1986). Profile of learning disabled persons in the rehabilitation program. *American Rehabilitation, 12,* 10–13.

Matza, D. (1969). *Becoming deviant.* Englewood Cliffs, NJ: Prentice Hall.

Mauser, A. J. (1974). Learning disabilities and delinquent youth. *Academic Therapy, 9,* 389–402.

McGrady, H. J. (1987). Eligibility: Back to basics. In S. Vaughn and C. S. Bos (Eds.), *Research in learning disabilities: Issues and future directions* (pp. 105–120). Boston: Little, Brown.

McGuinness, D. (1986). *When children don't learn.* New York: Basic Books.

McKinney, J. D. (1987). Research on the identification of learning disabled children: Perspectives on changes in educational policy. In S. Vaughn & C. S. Bos (Eds.), *Research in learning disabilities: Issues and future directions* (pp. 215–238). Boston: Little, Brown.

McKinney, J. D. (1988). Research on conceptually and empirically derived subtypes of specific learning disabilities. In M. C. Wang, M. C. Reynolds, & H. J. Walberg (Eds.), *Handbook of special education: Research and practice* (Vol. 2, pp. 252–281). New York: Pergamon Press.

Mehan, H., Hertweck, A., & Meihls, J. (1986). *Handicapping the handicapped: Decision making in students' educational careers*. Stanford, CA: Stanford University Press.

Mercer, J. (1973). *Labeling the mentally retarded*. Berkeley: University of California Press.

Mercer, C. D. (1987). *Students with learning disabilities*. Columbus, OH: Merrill.

Michaels, C. A. (1989). Employment: The final frontier. Issues and practices for persons with learning disabilities. *Rehabilitation Counseling Bulletin, 33,* 67–73.

Miller, J. L. (1990). Apocalypse or renaissance or something in between? Toward a realistic appraisal of *The Learning Mystique. Journal of Learning Disabilities, 23,* 86–90.

Miller, J. L., Mulkey, S. W., & Kopp, K. H. (1984). Public rehabilitation services for individuals with specific learning disabilities. *Journal of Rehabilitation, 50,* 19–29.

Minskoff, E. H., Sautter, S. S., Hoffmann, F. J., & Hawkes, R. (1987). Employer attitudes toward hiring the learning disabled. *Journal of Learning Disabilities, 20,* 53–57.

Mulkey, S. W., Kopp, K. H., & Miller, J. H. (1984). Determining eligibility of learning disabled adults for vocational rehabilitation services. *Journal of Rehabilitation, 50,* 59–63.

Murphy, R. F., Scheer, J., Murphy, Y., & Mack, R. (1988). Physical disability and social liminality: A study in the rituals of adversity. *Social Science Medicine, 26,* 235–242.

Murphy, S. T. (1988). Client and counselor views of vocational rehabilitation success. *Rehabilitation Counseling Bulletin, 31,* 185–197.

Murphy, S. T., & Salomone, P. R. (1983). Professional and client expectations of rehabilitation services. *Rehabilitation Counseling Bulletin, 27,* 81–94.

Murray, C. A. (1976). *The link between learning disabilities and juvenile delinquency: Current theory and knowledge*. Washington, DC: U.S. Government Printing Office.

National Association for Children with Learning Disabilities—Research and Demonstration Project (ACLD-R&D) (1978). *The link between learning disabilities and juvenile delinquency*. VA: National Center for State Courts.

National Joint Committee on Learning Disabilities. (1981). Learning disabilities: Issues on definition. *Journal of Learning Disabilities, 20,* 107–108.

National Joint Committee on Learning Disabilities. (1988). [Letter to NJCLD member organizations]. Author. Towson, MD.

Newill, B. H., Goyette, C. H., & Fogarty, T. W. (1984). Diagnosis and assessment of the adult with specific learning disabilities. *Journal of Rehabilitation, 50*, 34–39.

Nisbet, J., & Hagner, D. (1988). Natural supports in the workplace: A reexamination of supported employment. *Journal of the Association for People with Severe Handicaps, 13*, 260–267.

Oakes, J. (1985). *Keeping track: How schools structure irregularity.* New Haven, CT: Yale University Press.

Perlmutter, B. F., Crocker, J., Cordray, D., & Garstecki, D. (1983). Sociometric status and related personality characteristics of mainstreamed learning disabled adolescents. *Learning Disability Quarterly, 6*, 20–30.

Polloway, E. A., Smith, J. D., & Patton, J. R. (1988). Learning disabilities: An adult development perspective. *Learning Disabilities Quarterly, 11*, 265–272.

Ponte, M. R. (1974). Life in a parking lot: An ethnography of a homosexual drive-in. In J. Jacobs (Ed.), *Deviance: Field studies and self-disclosure* (pp. 7–29). Palo Alto, CA: National Press Books.

Poplin, M. S. (1984). Summary rationalizations, apology, and farewell. *Learning Disability Quarterly, 7*, 130–134.

Poplin, M. S. (1985). The reductionistic fallacy in learning disabilities: Replicating the past by reducing the present. *Journal of Learning Disabilities, 21*, 389–400.

Poremba, C. (1975). Learning disabilities, youth and delinquency: Programs for intervention. In H. Myklebust (Ed.), *Progress in learning disabilities.* New York: Grune & Stratton.

Public Law 94-142. (November 29, 1975). Education For All Handicapped Children Act. U.S. Congress.

Racino, J. (in press). Living in the community: Independence, support and transition. In F. Rusch, L. DeStefano, J. Chadsley-Rusch, L. Phelps, & E. Syzmanski (Eds.), *Transition from school to work for youth and adults with disabilities.* Sycamore, IL: Sycamore Publishing Co.

Rehabilitation Services Administration. (1981). *Memorandum from the task force on learning disabilities* (Information memorandum No. RSA-IV-81-39). Washington, DC: Author.

Rehabilitation Services Administration. (1985). *Program policy directive* (No. RSA-PPD-85-7). Washington, DC: Author.

Reynolds, M. C., & Wang, M. C. (1983). Restructuring "special" school programs: A position paper. *Policy Studies Review, 2*, 189–212.

Reynolds, M. C., Wang, M. C., & Walberg, H. J. (1987). The necessary restructuring of regular and special education. *Exceptional Children, 53*, 391–398.

Ried, B. (1984). Attitudes toward the learning disabled in the school and home. In R. Jones (Ed.), *Attitudes and attitude change: Theory and practice.* Reston, VA.: Council on Exceptional Children.

Rist, R. C. (1973). *The urban school: A factory for failure.* Cambridge, MA: MIT Press.

Rosenhan, D. L. (1973). On being sane in insane places. *Science, 179,* 250–258.

Rosenthal, I. (1989). Model transition programs for learning disabled high school and college students. *Rehabilitation Counseling Bulletin, 33,* 54–66.

Rosenthal, R., & Jacobson, L. (1968). *Pygmalion in the classroom: Teacher's expectations and pupils' intellectual development.* New York: Holt, Rinehart & Winston.

Ryan, W. (1971). *Blaming the victim.* New York: Vintage.

Sarbornie, E. J. (1983). A comparison of the regular classroom sociometric status of EMR, LD, ED, and nonhandicapped high school students. Unpublished doctoral dissertation, University of Virginia.

Schneider, B. H. (1984). LD as they see it: Perceptions of adolescents in a special residential school. *Journal of Learning Disabilities, 17,* 533–535.

Schneider, J., & Conrad, P. (1985). *Having epilepsy.* Philadelphia: Temple University Press.

Schur, E. M. (1980). *The politics of deviance: Stigma contests and the uses of power.* Englewood Cliffs, NJ: Prentice Hall.

Scott, R. (1969). *The making of blindmen.* New York: Russell Sage Foundation.

Senf, G. (1987). Learning disabilities as sociologic sponge. In S. Vaughn & C. S. Bos (Eds.), *Research in learning disabilities: Issues and future directions* (pp. 87–96). Boston: Little, Brown.

Seventh annual report to Congress on the implementation of Public Law 94-142: The Education of All Handicapped Children Act. (1985). Washington, DC: U.S. Dept. of Education, Office of Special Education.

Sharp, R., & Green, A. (1975). *Educational and social control: A study in progressive primary education.* London: Routledge & Kegan Paul.

Simpson, R. G., & Umbach, B. T. (1989). Identifying and providing vocational services to adults with specific learning disabilities. *Journal of Rehabilitation, 55,* 49–55.

Skrtic, T. M. (1986). The crisis in special education knowledge: A perspective on perspective. *Focus on Exceptional Children, 18,* 1–16.

Slavin, R., Madden, N., & Leavey, M. (1984). Effects of cooperative learning and individualized instruction on mainstreamed children. *Exceptional Children, 50,* 434–443.

Smith, C. (1983). *Learning disabilities: Interaction of learner, task, and setting.* New York: John Wiley & Sons.

Spear, L., & Sternberg, R. J. (1986). An information-processing framework for understanding learning disabilities. In S. Ceci (Ed.), *Handbook of cognitive, social, and neuropsychological aspects of learning disabilities* (Vol. 2, pp. 2–30). Hillsdale, NJ: Lawrence Erlbaum.

Stainback, S., & Stainback, W. (1984). The merger of special and regular education: Can it be done? *Exceptional Children, 51,* 2.

Stark, J. H. (1982). Tragic choices in special education: The effects of scarce resources on the implementation of Pub. L. no. 94-142. *Connecticut Law Review, 14,* 477–493.

Torgesen, J. K. (1987). Thinking about the future by distinguishing between issues that have resolutions and those that do not. In S. Vaughn & C. S. Bos (Eds.), *Research in learning disabilities: Issues and future directions* (pp. 55–64). Boston: Little, Brown.

Vaughn, S., & Bos, C. (Eds.). (1987). *Research in learning disabilities: Issues and future directions.* Boston: Little, Brown.

Vaughn, S., Bos, C. S., & Kucik, S. J. (1987). Moving from consensus to action: An agenda for future research. In S. Vaughn & C. S. Bos (Eds.), *Research in learning disabilities: Issues and future directions* (pp. 257–266). Boston: Little, Brown.

Wang, M. C., Reynolds, M. C., & Walbert, H. J. (Eds.). (1988). *Handbook of special education research and practice.* New York: Pergamon Press.

Wang, M. C., & Walberg, H. J. (Eds.). (1985). *Adapting instruction to individualized differences.* Berkeley, CA: McCutchan.

White, W. J. (1985). Perspectives on the education and training of LD adults. *Learning Disabilities Quarterly, 8,* 231–236.

White, W. J., Schumaker, J. B., Warner, M. M., Alley, G. R., & Deschler, D. D. (1980). *The current status of young adults identified as learning disabled during their school career* (Research Report No. 21). Lawrence: University of Kansas Institute for Research in Learning Disabilities.

Wiederholt, J. L. (1974). Historical perspectives on the education of the learning disabled. In L. Mann & D. Sabatino (Eds.), *The second review of special education.* Philadelphia: JSE Press.

Wilgosh, L., & Paitich, D. (1982). Delinquency and learning disabilities: More evidence. *Journal of Learning Disabilities, 15,* 278–279.

Wittrock, M. C. (1986). *Handbook of research on teaching* (3rd ed.). New York: Macmillan.

Wolfensberger, W. (1975). *The origin and nature of our institutional models.* Human Policy Press.

World Health Organization. (1980). *International classifications of diseases.* Ann Arbor, MI: J. W. Edwards.

Wright, B. A. (1983). *Physical disability: A psychosocial approach.* New York: Harper & Row.

Yesseldyke, J., Algozzine, B., Shinn, M., & McAve, M. (1982). Similarities and differences between low achievers and students classified learning disabled. *The Journal of Special Education, 16,* 73–84.

Zigmond, N. & Thornton, A. (1985). Follow-up of postsecondary age learning disabled graduates and drop-outs. *Learning Disabilities Research, 1* (1), 50–55.

Appendix

OUTLINE OF INTERVIEW QUESTIONS

1. Early recollections
   - testing/diagnosis
   - school
   - family issues
   - general activities
2. Elementary school
   - studies/specifics
   - teachers
   - friends
   - brothers/sisters
   - parents
3. Middle school/junior high
   - studies/specifics
   - teachers
   - friends
   - family issues
   - extracurricular activities
   - special programs
   - tutoring/accommodations
4. High school
   - studies
   - teachers
   - friends
   - family issues
   - extracurricular activities
   - special programs
   - outside tutoring
   - accommodations
   - college admissions/testing
5. College
   - selection of schools
   - admissions
   - early identification/detection

- special services
- accommodations
- relations with instructors
- study habits
- friends
- getting help
- thinking about work/career
- family relations
- special college

6. Graduate school
   - admission
   - testing
   - special services/accommodations
   - relations with instructors
   - getting help
   - thinking about jobs
   - internship experiences
   - social life
7. Employment experiences
   - descriptions of work history
   - selecting jobs
   - job interview planning/experiences
   - dealing with employers
   - doing the job
   - accommodations
   - getting help
   - co-worker/supervisor relations
   - job successes/failures
   - figuring out what I could do
8. Family issues
   - parents and siblings

- feelings about how they handled situation
- spouses
- children

9. Social issues
   - reactions of others to problems
   - telling friends (when, where)
   - boy/girl friends
   - handling questions/kidding

10. Technical assistance
    - adaptive equipment
    - special tutoring/instruction
    - medical interventions
    - psychosocial services
    - specialized personnel

11. Psychological issues
    - self-perceptions
    - thinking about myself in relation to others
    - coping with doubt
    - sources of support
    - changes in self-perceptions

12. Adult issues
    - thinking about problems as an adult
    - do the problems go away/less or more emphasis
    - relations with others
    - personal understandings and definitions

Index

About the Author ────────────────

Stephen Murphy is a native of West Hartford, Connecticut. He graduated from Holy Cross College in 1966, and received his Ph.D. in 1973 from the State University of New York at Buffalo. Currently, Dr. Murphy is an Associate Professor in the Division of Special Education and Rehabilitation at Syracuse University. His most recent research has focused on community integration and employment issues for people with disabilities. He has also written extensively on how people with disabilities view disability, the professionals with whom they work, and the services they receive.

Before coming to Syracuse, Dr. Murphy worked as a psychologist at the Veterans Administration Hospital, Lyons, New Jersey, and as an Assistant Professor of Education at the University of New Hampshire, Durham, New Hampshire. Recently, he took a partial leave from his faculty duties to become Executive Director of The Pioneer Agency Inc., a local sheltered workshop which he helped convert to a completely integrated employment service for people with disabilities.

Professor Murphy lives in Syracuse, New York, with his wife, Nancy, and their three children.